100 Days
On The
High Mountains
Of Character

100 Days On The High Mountains of Character

BERYL NYAMWANGE

Copyright © 2014 by Beryl Nyamwange.

ISBN: Softcover   978-1-4931-4268-2
            eBook   978-1-4931-4269-9

All rights reserved. No part of this book may be reproduced or transmitted in any form or by any means, electronic or mechanical, including photocopying, recording, or by any information storage and retrieval system, without permission in writing from the copyright owner.

Any people depicted in stock imagery provided by Thinkstock are models, and such images are being used for illustrative purposes only.
Certain stock imagery © Thinkstock.

This book was printed in the United States of America.

Rev. date: 05/29/2014

To order additional copies of this book, contact:
Xlibris LLC
0-800-056-3182
www.xlibrispublishing.co.uk
Orders@xlibrispublishing.co.uk
516573

CONTENTS

1. THE LEVEL 15
2. KEEPERS OF THE AQUARIUM 18
3. THERE IS 20
4. AUTHENTICITY 21
5. THE BUG OF INSPIRATION 23
6. A FIRE WITHIN 25
7. DAUGHTER OF THE KING 27
8. THE CHAMPION OF THE RACE 29
9. WHO HAS YOUR ATTENTION? 31
10. THE PEARL OF GREAT PRICE 33
11. GRIPPED BY URGENCY 35
12. MAY YOU FEED A HUNGRY WORLD
    THROUGH ME 37
13. LIKE A SHINING ROAD INTO THE FUTURE 40
14. QUICK FIXES 42
15. MY EMPLOYER 44
16. THE GIFT GIVER OF GIFTS 46
17. THE GOD SPACE 48
18. THE BRIDGE 50
19. THEY ARE WAITING 53
20. I WANT TO DIE 55
21. THE HAND THAT PLANTED THE GARDEN 59
22. A MARKET FOR CRACKED POTS 61
23. WONDER-FULL 64
24. A SPECIES IN THE INTENSIVE CARE 66
25. A NAME CHANGE 68
26. WHAT YOU SEE 70
27. I WONDER WHAT HE SEES 72
28. OF WEAVINGS 74
29. MY CHRISTIAN EXPERIENCE 76
30. SHE IS MY "ANOTHER" 79

31.	THE ARMY	85
32.	SOMETIMES I FORGET	87
33.	WHEN JESUS COMES TO STAY	89
34.	FINDING TREASURES	91
35.	A SANDWICH ON MY FRONT SEAT	93
36.	THE ONLY SUNSHINE I SEE	95
37.	THE CEMENT OF THE SOUL	98
38.	LET REASON RESUME HER OFFICE	100
39.	THE MAN OF THE HOUR	102
40.	AT THE BOUNDARY	104
41.	CONFORMED OR TRANSFORMED	107
42.	THE TENTACLES OF PRIDE	108
43.	PICKING AT STRAWS	110
44.	EAGER VOICES FROM THE PRISON OF FREEDOM	112
45.	THE FACTORY OF DIVINITY	114
46.	A MODEL	116
47.	SOAKED INSIDE THE OCEAN OF YOUR LOVE	119
48.	CAST YOUR NET ON THE RIGHT SIDE	121
49.	THIS DISEASED MIND	123
50.	UNDER CONSTRUCTION	124
51.	BURN THE CHAFF	126
52.	GRATITUDE APTITUDE	128
53.	LITTLE WALLS	130
54.	THE MIDDLE SEAT	132
55.	"HEARTITUDE"	134
56.	GOD'S BUSINESS	136
57.	FROM WHENCE HAVE I BEEN CUT?	138
58.	FINDING YOUR NICHE	140
59.	I AM ME!	142
60.	AM I A LIGHT BEARER?	144
61.	SPIRITUAL SEWERAGE	146
62.	FORGIVENESS IS A KEY	148
63.	CRUCIFY THE FLESH IN ME	150
64.	SHUT THE DOOR TO TEMPTATION	152
65.	VICTIMIZED OR VICTORIOUS	154
66.	A DISTINCT SOUND	156
67.	CONSTRUCT A BRIDGE	158
68.	THE ANAEMIC CHRISTIAN	160
69.	A LINK IN THE CHAIN	162

70.	THE CANDLE ON MY HAND	164
71.	THE VOLTAGE OF GRATITUDE	167
72.	ON MOTHER'S KNEES	169
73.	DON THE SACKCLOTH	171
74.	TRAITORS WITHIN	173
75.	THE TUMOUR OF UNFORGIVENESS	176
76.	LIGHTING A FIRE AT LAODICEA	178
77.	THE SNAIL CLASSROOM	181
78.	FASHIONED	183
79.	LESSONS FROM THE POTTER'S HOUSE	185
80.	THERE IS A FLY INSIDE THE OINTMENT	187
81.	WORDS ARE BUILDING BLOCKS	189
82.	THE JOYS OF BEING A WIFE	191
83.	MY DEATHLY PRIDE	193
84.	PURITY, YOUNG WOMAN/MAN!	195
85.	WALK THE ROYAL ROAD	197
86.	PRECIOUS JEWELS	199
87.	POWERFULLY TINY	201
88.	CHRIST—THE PILLAR OF ALL STRUCTURES	203
89.	LEGACY MOMENTS	205
90.	THE GOLDEN THREAD	207
91.	THE UNCOMFORTABLE CHRISTIAN	209
92.	I AM STILL CLIMBING	211
93.	GRIEF HAS A FACE	213
94.	ENDURANCE IS THE WELL MARKED PATH	215
95.	LEGACY	217
96.	THE BLEEDING VICTIM	219
97.	WHAT WRITING TEACHES ME	222
98.	FOUNDATIONS LAID	225
99.	I WANT	227
100.	THE FACES AND PHASES OF MOTHERHOOD	229

PREFACE

Welcome to 100 Days On The High Mountains of Character.

I have enjoyed a wonderful writing journey since my childhood. My parents seemed to understand when I marked walls and light bulbs with any kind of ink or crayon I came across. With each passing year, the passion for writing has continued to increase. I love it!

Join me in this journey to delightful discoveries from simple daily experiences. This being my first collection of 100 poems in one book at the time of this publishing, I trust that we will meet again "in thought" and hopefully face to face, as you read other encouraging poems, quotes and writings along the way: over 1,300 at the moment.

I want you to know that life is precious. Each new day, I jump into the joys of sunlight with the exuberant energy from the Holy Spirit, and when He makes me jump, He makes me jump high! He lifts me high above the world and its challenges. He wakes me up real good! He opens my eyes to see beyond circumstances to His holy vision for me. May this be a shared experience between you and I. As we journey on together, I pray you find solace, encouragement, correction, advice, delight, wonder, deep thought, questions, new lessons and much more from this little gift to your heart.

~Sincerely in words that transform~

~Beryl Nyamwange.

DEDICATION

My heartfelt thanks go to My Dad—Benjamin Aseno Odieny—a man after God's own heart, who taught me from my tender years that God is good. Dad, it's amazing how in my first few impressionable years of life, I thought you were God! Your gentleness, your prayerfulness, and your love to me—oh, these beautiful pointers to me of your character, convinced me beyond any reasonable doubt that you were the God that people worship, until you took time to show me that there is the Father in heaven as each night on your shoulders we counted the stars and smiled back at the moon, and we went to church every Sabbath and were taught at the cradle roll and kindergarten. Thank you for being one of life's precious gifts to me.

Mom, thank you for your tender loving care, your neatness in the home that made the home environment ever so pleasant! Your patience with a strong willed child like me is laudable!
I remember the days when my hands rest from writing on any surface available. You are the best health conscious cook, after me!

My dear brother, George Aseno, in whom I learnt early the joys of reading as you merrily shared your new discoveries from the Bible, Daniel and Revelation, and other Christian literature, whetting my appetite to want to find out for myself.

Dr. Risper Awuor: Mom's best friend in my childhood. You taught me in Kindergarten, and again in my first year as a University student. You will always be one of my role models as I have watched you aim higher and higher for God's glory. Your passion is contagious!

Dr. Emmanuel D. Mbennah; you were my Professor and Thesis advisor for my Master's degree in Communication. I studied at your feet the communication principles that have helped to give more strength to this book and many more to come.

My heartfelt appreciation goes to my beloved husband Joe. Joseph, thank you so much for your words of encouragement along the way. You saw me draft poems at church when we were growing together in the youth group. I gave them to you to read. You wrote notes beside them and gave your kind comments; all of which I have faithfully stored in a file to date. As I read those comments, I know that you have been supportive all the way. Your prayers and the blissful home we now enjoy together as a family have made this all the more possible, a joyous journey hand in hand indeed. God bless your heart my darling!

Where would I be without You, O my King and Savior, for in You alone do we get the gifts that You have apportioned to each of your children. It is You who has impressed my heart to do this work. To You be glory, honor, power, and majesty. Above all, thank You for preparing a place for me in Your heavenly kingdom, and I know that soon, I shall see You face to face. Thank You, My Jesus.

CHARACTER POEMS

The content in this book is about us and Him: Our Character. As you read through this "Character Piece," the poetry will draw your heart to want to be more like the One who is More than a Carpenter. He came to this earth in the form of a babe, born in a filthy manger; growing up in a poor house and surrounded by life in a poverty stricken neighbourhood. Yet His mission was clear and His agenda and calendar well marked with one goal: SALVATION FOR HUMANITY. Love for you and me!

It is to this Man of Character: Jesus Christ—that I am introducing you in these short pieces of poetry that bring out the reality of character so well. As you chew on each word, as expected of poetry lovers, and those that enjoy figurative language—and I think we all do as we read a script and "see"—you will see that His goal is to make us more and more like Him. In fact, He wants for us to have the "Mind of Christ." (1 Corinthians 2:16).

Each piece begins with a short summary of what the main lesson may be to you. You may find some little precious gems as you read through or a question that you may ponder over as you digest the content. At the bottom of each is some space where you may choose to write your own thoughts from a line or paragraph that best speaks to your heart. It is my earnest belief and conviction that as you read each, you will find a line or a paragraph that will speak to your heart directly. That is enough to give me joy in using this gift to encourage others.

May the poems help you to realize that we each have the Power from on High to make us better in our character journey and that each day; we will be enabled to do right because He took our place. He still comes to our rescue and shows us the right path.

This set is a wonderful small gift that you can share with loved ones for and during all seasons of life.

WELCOME!

We often like to say, "The ground is levelled" when we know we are up to something that in our strength we can accomplish. As you read this poem below, you will realize that this ground was levelled by blood! The hardened grounds of human hearts were soaked by blood make the ground soft for the ugly cross to stand tall and visible. He stretched His hands to the whole wide earth, and then He echoed loud: "I LOVE YOU!" His goal was and still remains: to save you and me. Welcome to the ground that is levelled.

1. THE LEVEL

The ground is flat
And unlevelled.
It is untidy
And filled with pebbles.
It is easy to trip and fall
And even get hurt.
And oft the sun beats
Upon the pebbles hot.

Through the rocky surface
A sculpture is fixed;
One made of mortals
Yet its message transfixed
Upon the mind to fathom.
It is a rugged piece of wood
And as many eyes upon this look,
They stop to linger and there remain.

On the wood is a heart
Beating with love extravagant
A heart descended from above,
To come down here and show love
To mortal creatures that on the wood
Did lay Him.

Pressed on the wood are hands
Stretched and opened wide
With joy exuberant;
Calling each one to come
For the strong grip
Of grace that is so abundant.

Clasped to the wood are feet,
That once toiled this earth;
Going places with power
To heal, seal and restore
Health and wellness
To them that walked
Where He was found.

On the wood are eyes
Winking with love;
Yet sometimes teary
For the soul
That refuses to look
Toward Him,
And He longs
With tender passion,
That soul to save.

On the wood are ears,
Listening with tender mercy,
To the plights and joys
Of His creation in agony;
He sends gentle whispers
Of peace to the hurting soul
And pulsations of joy on the journey.

On the wood are ribs,
Once pierced by cruel hate
Pouring forth blood and water;
The blood that saves
The water that cleanses.
Stabbed by men that He curved,
Yet embracing them still.

Nailed upon the wood are palms
Marked by a permanent sign;
Of that pain that drove the nail
Beyond the palms to the heart;
Causing love to be shone
Beyond the cross to the world
That His willing creation may
In eternity live with Him.

This unlevelled ground is levelled
By the hand of the One
Who on that cross did lay;
Crucified! Yet today,
He wants to level willing hearts
That no pebbles of sin be found
But His presence alone to abound.

Reflection Corner:

Visit an aquarium and realize how crucial it is that the workers are on time to feed the creatures in there. Cleaning has to be done on a regular basis to ensure all pipes allow oxygen to flow through and there are no blockages that may endanger the lives of the precious animals in there. We are keepers of the aquarium. Our task is clear. Now let us report to duty and keep watch!

2. KEEPERS OF THE AQUARIUM

An aquarium has been built,
By the largest hands that ever did exist.
The perimeter wall is vast,
And the water's overflowing fast.

The fish in the aquarium need oxygen,
Lest they die of suffocation.
They need a feeding program urgent,
For sustainable nutrition.

The fish in the aquarium are struggling
For fresh waters and breath;
For the aquarium is dirty and smelling,
And needs cleaning to the depths.

The rain of sin pelts through the aquarium,
And the coating algae of doubt affects the fish;
Causing the waters to be stinky and slimy,
And the fish slip.

The aquarium needs a revamp,
By the hand of Him alone who gives life.
He alone knows the expanse of the perimeters,
And can fill it with His abundant fresh waters.

Father, supply the oxygen of your grace;
Hearts to keep beating till we see your face.
Send food that never goes stale;
Spiritual nutrition that sustains.

Clean the depth where the algae of sin are stuck.
Clean the fish again and breathe within them a new.
Paint the walls of the aquarium with letters from your Word
And teach the fish your language to comprehend.

Finally, grow wings in the fish that they may fly
To the home; beautiful home you have prepared.
Not an aquarium where sin swims and lingers,
But green pastures where we sit face to face.

Reflection Corner:

Life has many components of things to do and things to hope for. People to love and people to comfort; evil to keep away from and good to run to. Peace to receive from the Source of Peace while the evil wants to tear us to pieces. Joy for the journey, yet some measures of encouragement to keep us focussed and steadfast. Calm amidst storms; showers of blessings and rains of despair. In all these, the choice remains ours. Which way shall we choose?

3. THERE IS . . .

There's a heaven to go to
And a hell to shun.

The Holy Spirit to listen to
And demons to flee.

The Lord to follow
And Satan to resist.

The Angels to guide us
And evil spirits to refrain.

The Bible to study
And earthly traditions to leave behind.

The praises of God to sing
And the voices of evil to refute.

The life eternal to look forward to;
The grave of death to conquer.

There are curses from him who bothers, yet
There's the Book with my name written perfect.

There's the one whose character I emulate,
And the one whose innuendos I regret.

Regardless of the challenges,
There are eternal blessings from our Father.

Reflection Corner:

In a fast paced world with so many price tags and big shopping malls, it is easy to lose focus on who we are, where we came from and where we are going. Eloquence demands that we have content, but here comes a new story! Sacrifice is willing to give us eloquence in His ways: ways that show us how to recognize our worth in Him, weighed in His scale and found not wanting when we follow in His ways. How authentic are you? How do you measure your authenticity?

4. AUTHENTICITY

May I be;

Authentic
In my identity in You.
Realistic
In my expectations of Your timing.

Perceptive
In my role in the lives of others.
Catalytic
In fulfilling Your mission.

Gigantic
In my vision of what You can do.
Sympathetic
With the weaknesses of others.

Loving
In my correction of others.
Optimistic
In my expectation of my future in You.

Watchful
In the cataclysmic view of world events.
Cosmic
In my treatment of all of Your creation.

Holistic
In my worldview.
May your sanity be mine
In my belief in You.

My abilities
Consecrated for Your use.
My humanity be pervaded
And possessed by Your divinity.

Reflection Corner:

We live in a beautiful capital city: Cape Town—with varying temperatures. During the summer, we have bugs all over and around us. It is picturesque to see butterflies showing off their obvious beauty, but it can be annoying when your kitchen sink is full of ants after your breakfast cereal bowls land in there! Bugs! Some are pretty, but they can also be annoying. Yet there is this kind of bug that bites and the bite is sweet, though not always timely. I call it the bug of inspiration—those moments when a "good idea" runs through the tracks of my mind and lands on my computer. What's your bug? Does it inspire you to be a better or a bitter person? I know One Source of Inspiration, and that is the Living Word.

5. THE BUG OF INSPIRATION

The bug of inspiration bites
At any time, at any moment.
It knows no time;
It takes up space in the mind.
It claims thoughts
And spreads like a wildfire in a forest.
It fires words at breathless speed
Its landing pool—a piece of paper.

The scribbles
Are full of great meaning,
Admonishing the falling,
Encouraging the weak,
Strengthening the feeble,
Guiding the lost,
Giving courage to the fearful,
Calming the anxious.

They bring relief to the oppressed soul,
Soothing the depressed,
Cheering the discouraged,
Gladdening the joyous,
Pitying the tender ones,
Carrying the broken-hearted,
Walking with the slow,
Encouraging us to keep going.

The bite of inspiration
Is never painful.
Yet it causes sweet agitation
That demands a place to stay put.
It pushes through the skin
Of thoughts to cleave,
And a visible outcome is seen
When it touches lives and weaves
A thread of power
With warps and looms of legacy,
That lasts beyond the present.

Inspiration outlives
The Inspired instrument;
Inspiration lasts
Beyond the moment.

Reflection Corner:

The sight of a burning fire often evokes two things: danger or warmth/safety. How so ironic? Think of sitting at a fire place during winter, or having a bonfire at night in the dark singing away. Think of being seated by a fire under a thatched roof through a cold night, or watching a house burning from a distance. All these stir up different emotions. Fire is powerful. As much as one spark can start warmth in the heart of humanity, another can yet be a sign of danger. There is a hand that ignites the right fire to the soul that is willing to be lit up with His presence. His fire can burn up enemies and cause warmth in the hearts of humanity.

6. A FIRE WITHIN

There is a fire within me,
Whose flames I cannot see.
The ignition is done by a majestic hand
Of Him who walked upon earth's sands.

This fire quenches sin's residue.
It changes me and makes me pure.
Ashes of depravity aren't left behind;
The Master cleans up all the filth He finds.

I feel His presence on my heart's corridors.
His giant steps are gentle and audible.
The fourth Man has appeared;
Knocking each door and oiling hinges unhindered.

Let the fourth Man in the flame be seen.
Let His works all eyes see and glean.
Let His voice through each space be heard.
Let Him gladden the strings and tune my heart.

Now for eager flames to come forth,
To be spurt out through my mouth;
Words from the throne room a heart to convict;
Songs of joy from heaven darkness to defeat.

These flames must spread a far;
Burn to ashes the vices that darken.
Gates of hell must remain a jar;
Conquered by the fiery voice from heaven.

Footsteps of the fourth Man doth linger
Within the flames; the Holy Spirit my Pathfinder;
Teaching me a soul to bring to His kingdom,
This fire from within me shines at His altar.

Oh for bright flames that spread beyond
This heart filled soul of mine to extend
The grace of warmth a soul to find;
Till on the table the fire prepares our land.

Reflection Corner:

Girls are special. Walk through a park filled with birds and squirrels and watch what the little girls do. They want these little creatures for pets. They want to hold them and cuddle them. They want to take them home. Girls become daughters and these become mothers and grandmothers. However, deep within us, we are girls! We don't seem to mind at what age we are . . . being called girls still is acceptable. Now, God has high standards for His girls. He gives them His name: Daughters of the King. If you are a daughter of the King, you know that He has great expectations of you and that He empowers you to live up to His honourable standards and He prepares us for the Holy City.

7. DAUGHTER OF THE KING

You ask me about my heritage.
Oh! I've got a long story to tell.
I once was lost but now I am found;
My story to give a certain sound.

I am a daughter of the King,
Empowered with a sweet song to sing.
He calls my name from His throne;
And on His palm is engraved my name.

Like the morning dew quiet and still,
His promises never fail.
When I hear the bird choir sing,
He wakes me up to visions higher.

Like the petals of the flowers bloom,
In His hands I have got room.
He patiently wipes the dews off my tears,
And lovingly says to me, "Do not fear."

My petals of joy face the rising Son.
His warmth beckons me to His altar come.
He keeps away the stings that cause me damage;
He allows those that grow me from age to age.

The rain of blessing falls upon my petals,
With thunderstorms of warnings loud.
For this petal must remain attached
To the branch lest the enemy attacks.

The wind of His Holy Spirit blows,
And I cannot afford a faltering brow.
His peace permeates the soil of my faith.
His roots send Living water my soul to bathe.

On the solid rock I remain grounded.
I stand erect on His word my pillar founded.
Producing a certain sound I must.
To Him I am eternally bound and cast.

When life's hailstorms my petals bruise,
Balm of Gilead will come to my rescue.
He keeps me free from the accuser.
I blossom where I am and His voice I hear.

Reflection Corner:

Olympics! This word comes to my mind when I think of races. In our individual lives, we each have a personal race we are running; something we are eager to achieve. Sometimes the eagerness outweighs the reality of the timing needed for the goal to be actualized. In fact, we run ahead, even of ourselves, and get disappointed when it dawns on us that our calendar is reading different dates from God's. Really, is completion the name of the game? Is it about getting to the finish line only? I think the process of running must be taken into account because it empowers the muscles to a finish that is well. So, whatever race you are running, enjoy being on the track. Yes, look to the prize, but enjoy each step of the race.

8. THE CHAMPION OF THE RACE

Amazing how fast-paced we all want to be;
Eager to achieve the price and the crown,
Oblivion towards all we need to see,
Desire to win may cause us a frown!

Is completion the name of the game
When in His mercies He calls us to bear
The burden of another; to wear His name,
And show that we care?

Slow me down in my attempts
To go before you and be tempted
To run ahead only to fall;
Only to fail.

Hiccups are welcome
If they will show me your path awesome
And warn me to stop and take a breath
That I may hear your voice clear and still.

It is not about winning,
But about following you.
It is not about conquering,
But trusting the Lord of the battle.

Be the champion of my race
As I run toward your face.
May the trophy I win
Be one free from sin.

May it come from your hand
With blessings you send
As I slow down
And let you give me a crown.

Henceforth take over my feet,
And show me where to fit;
That any encounters with defeat
Will be opportunities to bear fruit.

Reflection Corner:

Our attention is easily caught today by bill boards on the streets; news flash on the Television screen; advertising on various forms of media, fashion and Face book posts from friends and family. We are a very visual generation who appreciate pictures. We are a generation that needs to learn the value of silence. Yes, life is busy, even for a toddler because his or her needs must be met when he or she needs them. Life is busy for the retired one when all he or she has in the hands are numberless minutes that need to be used. So, who has your attention? Please find below some tips that will help you to not only survive in the "busyness" of life but to thrive at every moment of your living.

9. WHO HAS YOUR ATTENTION?

Life is busy nonetheless;
Many distractions more or less;
Who has your attention
Is the question.

This question an answer begs,
One that only you can provide.
On what is your attention pegged?
On whose side do you hide?

From materialism speedily run,
Her grip is but a temporary fun;
Yet with might it can hold you firm,
And dump her desires for you to yearn.

From dependence upon man flee.
His agenda coloured with the paint of self.
We are safer standing tall on our bended knee,
And the Rescue will come to our help.

On financial security do not depend;
Shifting economies that will soon end.
On the Father depend and allow Him to send
You to the highways with the salvation story to tell.

On physical beauty do not rely;
Mortal bodies where pain lingers with sighs;
Decay is evident save for His fruit in your heart garden;
There He plant seeds that last you until we meet in Eden.

Reflection Corner:

A pearl is a beautiful thing! How is a pearl formed? The birth of a pearl is truly a miraculous event. Unlike gemstones or precious metals that must be mined from the earth, pearls are grown by live oysters far below the surface of the sea. Gemstones must be cut and polished to bring out their beauty. But pearls need no such treatment to reveal their loveliness. They are born from oysters complete—with a shimmering iridescence, lustre and soft inner glow unlike any other gem on earth. Yet there is Someone more miraculous than a pearl! He purchased you and me at a great price—He died in order that we may have life.

10. THE PEARL OF GREAT PRICE

I have found the pearl of great price.
Not a jewel rare is He.
Available is He to all I realize.
This pearl has purchased me.

I have dug through the crevices of my mind;
Hoping this precious pearl to find.
I have pulled my hairs in wonder;
Believing I could find Him if I ponder.

I have squinted my eyes with hopes to see
This precious pearl in close proximity.
I have listened in utter silence,
Trusting the pearl to produce a sound intently.

I have raced through the garden in my backyard;
Turning stones and pulling off weeds.
I have on my bookshelf rearranged the cards,
Passionately seeking for the pearl in speed.

Yet the pearl has always been there;
This pearl has never moved!
He has arrived in my heart to take His place there;
Beating the entrance of my heart with a holy groove.

The pearl knows His mighty place,
And at the door of my heart He knocks.
I quickly open as He enters in to take shape;
My soil becomes rich and turns to a solid Rock.

This pearl is of a rock-strewn texture;
Firm enough to remain unbroken.
This pearl shines and my heart takes a picture;
It is the pearl on the cross once stricken.

This pearl is gentle in nature,
Fits into the curve of any human heart.
This pearl loves the dwelling of His obedient creatures,
His presence transforms my life to a fine work of art.

Reflection Corner:

Have you ever been gripped? Have you ever been dragged to an urgent meeting? You know how readiness was critical for the success of this urgency you found yourself in. The world we live in currently is on fast track: a race. We seem to be all running and chasing after something, some time or some food! But there is a kind of urgency that grips the soul that knows the world's destination. This urgency cannot be comfortable remaining seated on the church bench week after week. This urgency grips and sends us to the streets to help a soul find courage for the next day. This courage is available through the One who faced all the risks for us and in our place. Let us go forth with a sense of urgency for the mission we are in. Join my desperate soul for this delightful journey.

11. GRIPPED BY URGENCY

I am a desperate soul gripped by urgency
Of heaven and hell and their vivid realities;
Of souls groping in the darkness of sin's night,
While upon each page of the Word flickers light.

My desperate soul cries out for a brother,
Gripped in pain by the strong demon of addiction.
My desperate soul weeps out for a sister,
Strangled by the regrets of the act of abortion.

I see a teenager succumbing to peer pressure,
Virginity lost before the bright doors of marital bliss.
Hearts of children writhing in pain I cannot measure,
Emaciated for lack of love and with no keys to peace.

Shall I in idleness sit complacently and be desperate?
Shall the wellspring of my tears flow endlessly?
Is it too late?
Do I sense the urgency?

I am gripped by the urgency of grace;
He speaks and says, "All can see my face
If only you go to the highways and byways,
And bring them to dinner before it is too late."

I am gripped by the urgency of mercy;
Arms extended to bring comfort and relief;
To a soul on the brinks make happy;
Present before them life's precious gift.

I am gripped by the urgency of peace;
Puzzles of life begin to make sense
When the Potter takes the clay's broken pieces,
And stations them in the beautiful garden.

I am gripped by the urgency of love;
To all I am called to serve;
A hand extend to give an embrace;
The grace for all is always sufficient.

Reflection Corner:

Every day as we go out of our homes to work or to school, an inevitable sign greets us regardless of our kind of neighbourhood. This sign goes beyond affluence! The sign is visible in rich and poor communities. The sign is a human face—a hungry beggar on the street, asking for a dime or a piece of bread. Can God feed a hungry world through you? Has He put enough bread in your hands to share with those you meet? Has He given you His heartbeat so that the things that make His heart beat with love for humanity makes yours beat likewise? There is something more than daily bread. He is the Living Bread, and He wants to use simple people like you and me to feed a hungry world! He knows each need and His supply is abundant. Join in the Rescue Mission and let us feed a hungry world with all the Bread.

12. MAY YOU FEED A HUNGRY WORLD THROUGH ME

Oh the complacent walls that rise high
In the corners of our hearts;
Walls erected by our own impurities
When we feel it too much to do what you ask of us.

Alas! The wet floors where pity has been drowned;
Replaced by expensive tiles to make us comfortable;
Basking in the heat of our fireplaces,
When another is dying in the cold of the winds.

Oh the dust that creeps through our windows;
How fast we employ several to clean up our mess;
Afraid to make our friends think of us otherwise,
Yet this one has no place to lay her head tonight.

There is a hungry world at my gate;
Unborn children groaning in the heat of terminal illnesses,
For mother lacks the right source of nutrients,
To feed this unseen miracle growing inside of her.

There is a naked world at my gate;
Clothed in torn garbs that smell of compost,
For a teenager lacks a father to provide,
Clothes to cover his youthful nakedness.

There is an excruciating cry at my gate;
Tears of abandonment and uncertainty,
Of a young woman pregnant out of wedlock.
Did she miss out on parental guidance in childhood?

There is a sound of mourning at my gate;
Of a mother carrying her tender child,
Sick and in fever battling with HIV/AIDS,
The results of her rape encounter some time ago.

Where shall I run to
Answers to find?
Where shall I go to,
Someone to listen?

I am glad I need not go far;
For right where I am,
You are! You are! You are!
You are the one with the Father heart,
Who understands our disappointments and hurts.

To you I come with my questions,
For I am confident you have answers;
And though I may not comprehend all your ways now,
I know I shall see your grace active in and through me.

So one thing I ask of you
In answer to this prayer,
Is that you would use me
As your instrument to make a difference.

Feed a hungry world through me;
Not only with bread from the bakers,
But also with the Bread of Life from heaven's oven.

Quench the thirst of this world through me;
Not merely with water from the nearby river,
But with streams of Living Water from your throne.

Clothe this naked world through me;
Not just with clothes on sale from the distributor,
But with your robe of righteousness that never wears out.

Soothe a hurting world through me;
Not with soft music with earthly lyrics,
But with your Balm of Gilead that heals.

Comfort a world in pieces through me;
Not with a supply of all our wants,
But with an abundant supply of your peace.

So, here I give you my hands.
Use them for all these purposes;
To feed,
To clothe,
To soothe,
To comfort,
And to do immeasurably,
Yes; abundantly, above all
That you alone may receive the glory.

Here I am.
Let's go to work.
I am ready.
Use me.

Reflection Corner:

We are a world of travellers. Many are catching planes to various destinations for meetings, for family time, for vacations and even for medical attention. There are highways that are jam packed with cars every day, and we sometimes find ourselves in traffic for long hours as we wait to get home or to another destination. We get a sense of relief when as we journey, we finally arrive at our destination well and whole. Disappointments come when we hear of accidents or tragedies before the journey is over. Regardless, we are all travelling to some place. The question is, "WHERE?" The answer? Into the future—where the Driver knows the destination and takes us on this trip aboard His wings. Join in the journey.

13. LIKE A SHINING ROAD INTO THE FUTURE

I am on a journey.
Sometimes I go on foot
And I think myself slow.
Sometimes I fly in jets
Of fast paced human planes.
Sometimes I ride in our own car.
Sometimes I travel alone,
Sometimes I have company.

Yet one thing remains constant:
A forward looking view,
A yearning my destination to arrive,
A gathering of clouds to my front as I walk,
A cruising amidst clouds as I fly.

A road into the future is what I see.
It shines bright as my eyes behold;
Therefore, my longing for my destination
Makes the bumps but a very little inconvenience.

This shining road into the future
Is paved by the Master and His character;
Strong enough to endure any weight,
The driver patient enough the pedestrian to wait.

The raindrops of life wet this road;
They seem to slow me down;
Yet I choose to see them as blessings upon my path
To keep me safe from my personal agenda on earth.

I see flickering lights in peels of thunder;
The sound though scary and the lightning strikes,
I am reminded to fear not the distant trouble,
For my Driver has it all under control.

Sometimes rocks seem to block my entrance;
And I murmur about their presence,
Then my Driver faithfully whispers,
"This Rock blurs you from the enemy's view."

This road will shine brighter unto the perfect day,
When this piece of clod and clay that I am;
Will be welcome with the Master to stay,
And on the streets of gold talk with Him again and again.

Reflection Corner:

Those moments when a word would change a circumstance into providence! A tire burst! Dinner burnt on the stove while the family waits eagerly for it! Fire at a neighbour's house! A sick child in the middle of the night! Restless heartbeats at midnight in preparation for a job interview tomorrow! Someone's about to give birth to her first child! The days between now and my examination are getting shorter and I need to pass this test! The long awaited phone call from a loved one missed because someone's car had a tire burst in traffic and slowed every one down! That health issue that just needs to go away—like if we could blow cancer away! The list is too long! We like quick fixes and we want them now. But God works with His calendar and His agenda is perfect.

14. QUICK FIXES

God doesn't always major in quick fixes of situations;
For quick fixes tend to be a work done in a hurry;
A task that has outdated its original timing;
A process that ignores the joys of the journey
As it rushes to the destination unprepared.

My God prefers to work at His pace;
For He is the master of time;
Whose pace knows neither haste nor delay.
Whose plans always come to pass;
Whose design always shows the beautiful pattern.

He takes His time
To purposefully fix the squeak
That causes irritation to us.
Oh won't you be glad,
That He finally did it?

The big picture view?
He will give you.
You will confirm His methods;
You will approve of His motives;
You will be glad He did.

The outcome will be
For your own benefit.
You will see the big picture
That will eternally capture
Your grand reality of His character.

You will fulfil your mission.
You will receive new vision.
You will feel honoured to be His creation.
With His fulfilled intentions;
You will eventually arrive at your destination.

Reflection Corner:

The world population has continued to plummet and we are running out of jobs! So many people are looking for employment, and that first day on the job is often a scary one. On that day you get some orientation of the work environment and you begin a journey of discovery of who your boss is; with likes, dislikes, deadlines and other things. Sometimes there is the tendency to want to work overtime to please your boss, or to outdo others. Promotions always smell good until they go to someone else's space, and we realize the aroma is far from us. Nevertheless I have an employer whose work conditions are the best.

15. MY EMPLOYER

I work with a Boss who can never resign.
None will ever be found worthy to take His position.
My employer not only caters for my daily basic needs,
But has also given me the air I breathe.

I am not on a contract with Him,
For contracts expire.
Ours is an agreement;
A covenant that lasts forever.

Every day He wakes me up to go to work
And points me my tasks for each day.
When I am hungry and thirsty,
He is my Bread and my Living Water.

This employer does not only gift me with earthly dues
Which cause me to wonder—like fresh air, the gift of sight
And hearing and the ability to smell, touch and think—
But He also gives me life eternal.

He gives me one day off each week;
The Sabbath rest to fellowship with Him.
When I need sick leave, this Great Physician
Comes to my side to minister healing.

He is always right here with me to guide.
He never leaves my side.
He is daily teaching me to discern His voice.
Even when I am weary and tired and lost.

In sleep, He covers me with His protection,
He speaks to my mind His wonderful grace.
When I travel, He is my shield and buckler.
On the journey He remains my advisor.

When I am lost, He holds my hand
And brings me back to His direction.
He has never scolded or intimidated me.
Instead, He teaches me how to do my job.

He tells me I can work anywhere in the world.
I am never restricted to one place in fact.
He makes this possible because He is not limited
By space or time; He is limitless.

No one can fire me!
I am His permanent employee;
We keep in touch without a phone;
I am an heir of His kingdom.

He says that soon,
He is coming to give me
A brand new mansion,
That no eye has yet seen.

I am looking forward
To touching that mark on His palm;
Where my name is inscribed;
Hallelujah!

Reflection Corner:

We all love to receive gifts; well, at least most of us do. In fact, sometimes we expect gifts at certain seasons of the year. Is a gift worth receiving if the giver is not one dear to our hearts? The gift and the giver are often connected, but would there be a gift without a giver? In other words, in our pursuits for joy, we need to realize that there is a Source, and that source when tapped onto, brings other blessings in its train. Let me cherish the Giver of gifts more than the gift itself, and I will appreciate both and treat both with care and worth. This poem is like a narrative, and I hope you enjoy it as you read and meditate through.

16. THE GIFT GIVER OF GIFTS

On the vast desert of life I was,
When I stopped my Master to put to task.
"Didn't you say I should ask You for whatever I want?
"Didn't you say Your promises never to recant?"

Then I asked You for water to quench my thirst.
You gave me your well of abundance that lasts.
I asked You for bread for my hungry stomach.
You told me to use Your Living water for a harvest much.

I asked You for direction on my pathway in the night.
You pointed me to look up to the starry hosts and their light.
And as I followed Your twinkle; my face no longer in wrinkles
I arrived at the destination; with You in sole habitation.

At The Holy Ground You waited for me;
To sit, chat and commune with Thee.
You needed my friendship,
Yet for your gifts I yearned.

When at the Holy Ground we finally spoke,
I heard you enter my heart with a holy knock;
I knew I needed more of the Gift giver
Than the gifts He gives.

I learnt to be content;
But not the contentment of a mere receiver;
Selfish to gain wholly for myself,
Yet forgetting others to bless.

I needed friendships
To surround me with love.
You gave me your Holy ambience,
Undiluted from above.

I needed reassurance of who I am;
You reminded me you are the Great I am.
I needed my life's priorities reorganized;
You gave me the peace that never agonizes.

I needed my tears wiped and my needs met,
You gave me tears of joy and a new heartbeat.
I needed you more than any gift,
For in you alone is the whole gift.

It is all about YOU!

Reflection Corner:

The issue of space is one that we have all confronted at one point or another in our lives. Oh, the one that comes to mind is in the plane while flying. Where else to go? Just hang in there till the pilot says it's time to land. Sometimes in the plane as we all try to get seated, the arm of someone may knock you just a bit. Usually people are quick to apologize. Another issue of space that we confront is the child in the mother's womb. They have been "home" for nine months. Suddenly, they must be released to this cruel world. Often more than not, they all come out crying, not laughing or smiling. There is a sense of change they instantly feel. Yet I know a space that is safe. I call it the God space. Here the controls are sure and your release from the comfort zone is to usher you to increased "discomfort" that gives you peace; a peace that comes with increased comfort. Welcome to the God space.

17. THE GOD SPACE

The God space;
Where my abilities collapse,
At the realities of His possibilities.

Where my resources
Are meagre and scarce,
And I return to the source of all things.

Where my plans cannot succeed,
So that His plans can supersede,
As upon His cross I plead.

Where the key of faith opens miracle doors,
And obedience sees through its windows;
His Strength in my weakness.

Where clouds of doom
Shine forth lights of bloom,
In His holy room.

Where darkness turns to light,
And my temporary plight
Takes flight.

Where oceans of providence He parts;
Rocks of grace He cuts;
Sprinkles of Living water to impart.

Where the tongues of critics,
Slash not my abilities
But enables me to speak His lyrics.

Where the mighty arm,
Holds me to calm
As I cross the storm.

Where the stars under dark clouds shine;
Filters of grace from the divine;
I am His majestic design.

Where God surprises us
Beyond our inclinations
To maximize our limitations.

Where upon the altar lies a living sacrifice,
And the Father trusts the Son,
To provide the sacrificial lamb.

Where the presence of iniquities
Flee at the evidence of righteousness;
The Lord of glory weaves my life story,

Where obedience is key
To blessings received,
And the voice that bids
With gifts equips.

Reflection Corner:

Bridges are important. They make that which was impassable passable. They create a way where there seemed to be no way. In some countries there are bridges that are anchored across the ocean waters. Such are often mobile. They can move in order to allow the big ships to pass through, and upon them people walk. You have either crossed one walking or driving through. There is however a Bridge I know! This Bridge has made a way where there was no way. This Bridge connects earth to heaven; the heart of God to the heart of humanity. This Bridge moved so that man could pass from death to life. This Bridge remains mobile, available to the hearts of humanity. This Bridge allows all who desire to be saved from the drowning of sin, to be ferried safely to the other side. The Bridge is strong and can never break apart. It is the root to eternal safety. Come let us cross over before it is too late.

18. THE BRIDGE

From this side of my being,
I walk upon earth's dungeons.
Seems like sin everywhere clings;
The tumour inoperable by any surgeon.

Then my eyes behold the sign,
A rugged, dirty piece of wood.
Then my heart is inclined
To cross over and see what looms.

Right before me is a bridge;
Not curved by human hands.
It is not paid for by earthly wages;
This bridge never rests on sinking sands.

Though wooden and simple in my sight,
This piece of wood a holy purpose serves.
On this path I wait to take my flight,
For the hand from heaven guides me from above.

As this bridge I gently cross,
The mighty arm guides my footsteps.
I no longer cringe nor get tossed,
But determinedly follow His steps.

The strength of the wood is stained in blood.
This stream sends upon my soul loving floods.
I cross over to the safe side,
Secured from sin's flaming tides.

The bridge is fixed by living nails;
Unshaken by human force.
The power of the bridge upon the soul sails,
As I constantly look to the Source.

A voice echoes from the bridge;
A crown of thorns the bearer adorns it.
The voice breaks sin's ridge
That Satan upon the heart fixed.

Seems like an accident on the bridge
But it is not fatal.
Though the victim is on the edge,
Yet not cast after all.

As the victim bleeds to death,
His blood sends life to earth.
All the willing passersby who like the stain,
Will have the life of the victim that burdens lighten.

The scene of the accident is cleared.
The victim is resurrected.
I stand amazed at His love.
To Him I am reconciled.

Grace upon this bridge is fully painted
With colourful hues of forgiveness for the weary sojourner.
Mercy upon this bridge is extravagantly out laid;
Secured from death is the traveller's future.

Feet that trod this sod once screwed;
A place of safety now prepared for me.
This weary sinner in need of repentance
Now walks this earth by grace and faith in Him.

Reflection Corner:

Life is about waiting. The night waits for day. The day waits for night. Summer waits for winter, and winter comes for sure. We all wait each day for something or someone. It is inevitable. Life is a wait a minute—a wait! The waiting journey has various signs on the way. Sometimes we get to them and grumble, and sometimes we are in a hurry to pass the red light. However, there is a kind of waiting that I find very uncomfortable; at least to me—based on what I have seen of them that wait in this manner. This is a waiting that longs for your touch of warmth and love; your voice of cheer and grace; your whisper of hope and your encouragement for the journey ahead. They are waiting. For you! For me! Come to the streets, or walk through prison doors. Come to the dungeons and corners where drugs are sold. They are waiting. For you! For me.

19. THEY ARE WAITING

They are waiting;
For our welcome through the open doors of our hearts and homes.

They can't read our thinking;
They just hope we will respond with compassion.

They are looking;
Hoping to spot a loving mother or a caring father.

They are trusting
You and I not to run away any further.

They are believing
That one of us cares enough their talents to spot.

They are living
Each day with the expectation that their dreams will never rot.

They are vulnerable,
Often afraid and voiceless.

They hope we are available;
They hope we consider them jewels priceless.

Who will gently hold their tiny hands?
Who will tap into their growing wisdom?
Who will the flame of their desires fan?
Who will rescue them from the world's doom?
Who will watch out for danger as the streets of life they cross?
Who will guide their feet as they deal with life's losses?
Who will point their eyes in the direction of priorities?
Who will strengthen their hearts to grow their abilities?
Who will speak the language of their souls?
Who will lift their faith up when they slide and fall?
Who will water the seeds of goodness within them?
Who will weed out the thistles that prick them?
Who will shine the light on their paths at dusk?
Who will respond to the great questions they ask?
Who will soothe their gaping wounds?
Who will listen to their unspoken sounds?
Who will teach them principles good?
Who will provide them with daily food?
Who will be present when they call?
Who will show them the source of life eternal?
Who will?
Will you?

Reflection Corner:

Death is that final enemy that we can't wait to see defeated. It robs us of loved ones and brings us memories that are hard to deal with. It steals away precious moments of our lives and leaves us wondering what could have been. It cares less about age or status, but that it captures the victim, often unawares. I have good news for you; one that death cannot steal away. The news is that there is a kind of death that all must invite. This death releases us to new life. It removes from our congested lives unnecessary strife and causes us to triumph. This death is one we must seek for and yearn to have happen in our hearts! It is a daily dying. Oh that this death would come to all of us sooner than later. Do you want to die this death? Read on. It is one without a funeral. No tears, no mourning. Just joy and dancing; dead yet fully alive!

20. I WANT TO DIE

Lord, today I want to die.
Today, I welcome the grave of death.
I am ready to be buried beneath.

It is not a kind of death
Caused by an assassination;
Triggered by mortal hands.

It is not a kind of death
That happens upon me suddenly
As a result of a stray bullet.

This death is not due to an epidemic
Of eminent proportions
In my vicinity.

It is not a death after many years
Of the lingering wounds
Of a fatal disease.

This death is not brought about
By a road accident;
The lethal mistakes of a careless driver.

It is not a death
Instigated by what we know
As natural disasters.

No, this death is not one
That lends the human face
A flood of tears;

In fact, this death gives energy
To the heart and mind;
It makes the whole being beat with life.

It is the grave of self
That you dig deep, deep beneath
I ask you to bury me under.

It is where mortals find resurrection
In the life of the immortal One.
It is where mortals win.

It is where the breath of life
Breathes life into our dying selves.
Where sin no longer dominates.

It is where the Resurrected One
Beckons us arise!
We stand up to meet the standards.

It is not one dug by human mortals in pools of tears;
But one tunnelled by the hand that can cleanse my heart's chambers;
A hand that searches the deep things in the core of my soul.

Gently and often painfully, it scoops out the unwanted residue,
And leaves me pure and clean with Him my life to subdue.
I learn to recognize His holy and timely cues.

This grave is not covered with decaying flowers;
But one whose layers are made of crowns of thorns.
No, I am not descending lower!

These crowns of thorns germinate
To bear Christian flowers of grace;
Whose petals beauty life with holy scent.

A grave Lord, not cemented
By bricks from human factories.
But of walls made strong by the Pillar of Life.

A grave smeared by the eternal blood.
Where no face is no longer sad,
For hearts rejoice in His deeds good.

This is the death I want to die!

Lord today I welcome the grave of death.
Not one covered by human insurance,
But one prompted by the cross;
Proven by your abundant love evidences.

Who can kill me in this way?
None but you Father!
So, destroy the self in me;
Bury her beneath and bury her deep.

I must confess that she has the tendencies
To bring up her stubborn head;
To want to look good in the face of humanity;
To want to show forth her pitiful works.

Clothed in the ruggedness of unrighteousness,
Her eyes fill with clods of judgment of others.
Her ears block from the echoes of grace.
Her nose fails to smell the aromas from heaven.

Oh she needs a thorough brain clean up.
A cleansing of these mental faculties;
Not done by human cloning or genius making;
But pierced by the Sword of your Spirit.

But this is not about her Lord,
For when you kill me, I am dead to sin
I am alive to Jesus Christ my Lord.
Now and forever more.

So, bring forth your sickle;
Start digging my grave
By uprooting those stubborn weeds
Of flaws in my character;

Those dying leaves of impatience.
Those stems that are bent over towards sin and wickedness.
Those petals that are decaying in the heat of compromise.
Those pods flown away by the winds of carelessness.
These, uproot, burry and resurrect me
To eternal purity and life forevermore.

New waves of holy thoughts to spring forth.
New mercies of love upon others to share.
New graces ever gaining with each step.
New desires growing in the soil of faith.
New sympathies for this fallen world.
New energies to stand up and serve.
New messages received from heaven.

This is the death I want to die!

Reflection Corner:

Gardeners are precious people. What would we do if not for the energies they employ so we see fruit and enjoy? They are happy to get dirty on the outside so we can get clean in our insides—washed by the fruits and vegetable juices the gardens they tend bring forth. However, there is this Gardener whose work excels all. He created the first garden and planted the first fruit trees. Until now unto eternity, He has the on growth and how it happens. His hands were pierced by those He fed. Those hands bear an eternal mark upon them, yet they hold me close to Him each day. These hands are long enough to encircle the world and embrace each child of His. These hands soothe and comfort. Today He beckons you, "Come unto Me."

21. THE HAND THAT PLANTED THE GARDEN

The hand that planted the garden;
This strong arm of diligence
Carries all my burdens,
And sprinkles me with guidance.

This hand encircles the world
With love from the throne above.
It is the hand of a mighty God
Stretched forth with chords of love.

Pierced, He bore pain with patience.
His grip upon mankind determined.
He hung on that old rugged cross;
My soul to save with imminence.

This hand soothes my pain;
Directs me to the path of gain.
He anoints my head with oil,
A sanctified being He moulds.

This hand weeds my heart garden;
Removing the thistles that prick my character.
He spreads forth a fertilizer that never weakens,
But strengthens my crop to a bumper harvest.

This hand folds mine when I am in prayer;
Helps me feel the touch of my fingers
Clapping to the witness of His power,
As He makes me on life's street a singer!

This hand touches my head when I need rest;
He lays a table for me when I need a feast.
He pulls back my chair and shows me my seat,
He presents me an eternal treasure and gifts.

This hand is stained with living blood
That rushes through my veins to restore;
Gives me a table filled with living food,
Prepares me for life's battles and woes.
This hand holds me at my workplace;
Helps me to walk according to His pace,
He lifts my countenance and says
"Stay with me and you won't lose your gaze."

This hand is returning to pick me up;
To show me how to fly to the eternal home.
He calms my heart and my body wraps;
This hand has an engraving marked, «welcome!»

Reflection Corner:

We are earthen vessels indeed; created by the hand of a Master and brought forth to a world in need. He could have sent millions of angelic hosts to complete this work, but no, He sees it fit to work with cracked pots because He knows how to fix each. However fragile each pot is, He has the right material. He own all time. He is dedicated to fixing these pots so that the new design can glaze to reflect His eternal beauty. Today, are you feeling cracked by life's heat of trailing circumstances, one after another? Are you torn by tough decisions that seem to have no conclusions? You are not the only pot with visible cracks. We are many in the Potter's house, and His tools are arranged to help us regain our original design. Cracked pots must still go to work. No excuses. So, do what a cracked pot does. Stay at the Potter's house and watch Him mould you!

22. A MARKET FOR CRACKED POTS

Fragile, fallible, yet functional and *fillable*.
A treasure hidden in this earthen vessel;
Often stressed by the heat of life's daring flames;
It cracks and sometimes definitely unreliable.

Brittle, this clod of clay.
Wrapped in simple and aging layers of skin.
Bleeding from the wounds of life's days.
Wondering if there is any price to win.

Easily broken this piece of clay is.
Smashed by a word carelessly spoken.
Wounded by a negative thought gone amiss.
Bruised and fettered, yet remains chosen.

Fallible in the wisdom of life's choices.
Prone to wander, prone for big mistakes.
Vulnerable and easily falls for doom's doses.
Yet the breath of life at high rising stakes.

Functional, even though often weary and tired.
Bogged down by the weight of life's atrocities.
Though to help another the heart is wired,
Yet how often discouraged by pain's shouting realities.

Oh, what wonder!
Oh, what mystery!
Of grace to ponder,
Deliverance from misery!

Earthen vessels we all are;
Baked in the heaven's undying oven;
Weak, unsure, tired and frail,
Yet Father has paid a market price for vessels broken.

Each vessel He gently holds between His hands;
Each He moulds for a super work grand;
Mends the cracks and repairs the broken pieces,
Sends forth the vessel to show forth the face of Jesus.

Remember, you are not the only lump
Of clotted clay around here;
We are all in God's pottery camp
And He is shaping each layer.

Angels could have been His choice and pick,
To show humanity the face of Jesus.
Disqualified they were when He took the risk,
To use a broken, earthen vessel to display His grace.

Cracked pots that we are;
We are God's choice.
In His warehouse are all tools for repairs,
His wind instruments to echo His voice!

He wants to keep us ready for surprises.
Through our cracks He passes His infilling,
And we fully His promises embrace;
This earthen vessel obeys God's biddings!

A piece of ordinary humanity that I am,
The Potter has chosen me His face to show.
I fear not as I listen to the voice of the Great I am,
Filling this earthen vessel with wisdom o'er and o'er.

In my fragility;
You are my utmost ability.
I tend to break,
But these earthen pieces drop, you remake.

Fallible and often wrong,
Yet deep inside this pot echoes a song.
Soothing tunes to be shared with a world gone wild;
To alleviate the aches and another vessel guide.

Functional, but often not deep enough
For roots to penetrate to the core.
Though the earth's surface be rough,
I know I am a treasure in your earthen store.

Fillable, yet with evidences of leakages.
You do not give up on this visible wreckage.
Your love has made an eternal pledge;
A commitment that has chosen me through the ages.

Reflection Corner:

In a very busy world, where cell phones track our whereabouts and emails seem to whisper, "come attend to me now or else . . ." we find ourselves always busy with a gadget or two in hand. We live in a world of sin, and relationships are breaking each day, but hope is not about to give up. No. Hope is here to stay and that hope is evident in the beautiful glimpses we have each day of life in its beauty. We just need to stop and soak in those moments of wonder! When a baby cries with such innocence; when a sick patient is struggling to breathe and we stop to thank God for the life and not question Him about the pain; when you escape being the victim of a tragic accident; when you lose a leg but not a life, these are precious. These moments of wonder are wonder-full, and if only we care to look we will find plenty each day. Now, welcome to a wonder-filled day.

23. WONDER-FULL

Make each day a wonder-full day.
Let common things remain uncommon;
The raggedy rock on your walk and pathway;
Can it preach you a sermon?

Do not iron out the wrinkles of uncertainty;
Instead, let them steam your pot of curiosity,
Then as each crease of the day gently unfolds,
The cloth of your expectation will show forth hues bold.

Flatten not the peaks of wonder and surprise;
Do not dig out her roots at sunrise.
With a sickle of hope each day curve out moments,
To reflect upon life's designs and learn from her patterns woven.

Be awed by the whispers of the morn's still air.
Join the choir of the birds in the sweetest tunes.
Drape your retina with the beauty of the hill's peaks and layers.
Bury your feet of peace in life's daily sandy dunes.

Enjoy the miracle of little feet run across the street.
The sounds of school children at play;
The calm river by the rocky side, dip your feet.
Your moments will hence know no decay.

Tantalize yourself with tickles of creativity.
Let laughter be your snack of energy and joy.
Be enamoured by the variety among the human species;
You will find nothing your thoughts to annoy.

Respect the mystery of each passing minute.
Activate your imagination as the clock chimes.
Learn eternal lessons through periods of defeat.
Your wonder-full life more worthy than sacks of dime.

Transcend your lust to have everything under control.
Let the doors of wonder and miracle burst open on your face.
Accept each day as an opportunity for growth to bud.
Can your imagination upon the hues of the sunset glaze?

Allow your jaw to drop, your eyes to pop, your knees shake.
Relax and be reduced to simple amazements.
Squeeze your hands together and feel the power they make.
Go forth and live your life in total engagement and commitment.

Reflection Corner:

Created perfect and in harmony with the heart of God Himself; purity glazed upon their existence in the garden. Their countenances beamed with sparks of elation. Then it took just one step to a downward spiral. It seemed like a simple conversation, but it was with the wrong crowd at the wrong time. What followed was a messed up chain of thoughts entangling the pair. The subtle serpent came to Eve with questions and doubts when she thought a walk on her own would bring some relief. The pair soon sensed something was wrong, and so did their Creator. He came calling out "Adam, where are you?" Not that He did not know where they were; He did. Why then? This pair needed to realize that death came through their door. Thanks to God, He rescued us from intensive care and is creating mansions for them that believe and will hush away the serpent's voice. Lord, have mercy upon this generation of ours.

24. A SPECIES IN THE INTENSIVE CARE

Male and female
He created them;
To fan His eternal flame;
Then the fire of doom fell.

Into the garden
He allowed them entrance;
Then His countenance they saddened,
When they embraced offense.

Now a species
In intensive care
Where life's not easy
And moments of joy rare.

A species in intensive care
Where the Father Surgeon
With His scalpel of love must dare
Come to our rescue before life's gone.

In His intensive care,
On the bed of humility I must lay,
For He alone shows me where
I ought to be by night and day.

In His intensive care, a banner over my wounds.
He to awaken me from this anaesthesia;
Before the trumpet sounds;
This love to me dares.

The nurse of hope to my bedside doth come.
My frail fingers to flip open His word.
Sin's tumours in my heart He burns.
My oxygen beyond now He affords.

This species never to go extinct;
For before the foundation a plan
Was laid; humanity's purpose succinct
And on the cross all said and done.

The species multiplying He must;
For the heavens the creator repopulate.
Though sinners, the species not an outcast
But heirs His character to emulate.

The species not a crossbreed of sin,
But His own pure blood within.
In His image and likeness made,
Shining His light in darkness of day.

Transfer this species to the recovery ward;
Where his wounds you observe and record
So he may heal fully,
In readiness for an eternity healthy.

Let his illness another not contaminate.
The time of quarantine must quickly pass
That the recovery process may germinate
Seeds of character with pools of grace.

Reflection Corner:

Who wants a name change? Not unless you are called "Judas," I suppose. Names are an integral part of our identity that we can never run away from. We are born and given names, and these last with us our life time. When someone calls my name, I respond. Names help to identify us in various records and they facilitate the process of finding our details where necessary. Sometimes we may choose to change our names depending on certain factors; for example, when we get married. Yet our first records show the original names. Names are important. There are others though, in our world today with names we have given them—names hard to pronounce. These include, "homeless, estranged, ignorant, abused," and the list goes on. There is good news however! God wants to give us a new identity, a name change that no one can change. He wants to transform us so that our names are not only changed, but written in His Book of Life forever. I am ready for a name change. How about you?

25. A NAME CHANGE

You need a name change?
God wants to change your name.
From abused to adopted.
From abandoned to accepted.

From bruised to blessed.
From bewildered to begotten.
From crushed to colossal.
From cursed to crowned.

From doomed to delivered.
From disobedient to diligent.
From estranged to esteemed.
From embittered to exonerated.

From fearful to free.
From fallen to fruitful.
From gruelling to great.
From gruesome to good.

From helpless to hopeful.
From homeless to hired.
From irritable to innocent.
From ignorant to intelligent.

From a jerk to a jewel.
From kaput to kinfolk.
From loathed to loved.
From loose to longed for.

From miserable to magnificent.
From moody to melodious.
From nothing to newness.
From niggardly to nice.

From obstinate to orderly.
From poor to persistent.
From plain to pious.
From queer to queen.

From restless to restful.
From rascal to revived.
From silly to stupendous.
From sabotaged to surrendered.

From trampled to terrific.
From tough to tender.
From unknown to unsurpassed.
From unloved to unrivalled.

From vain to value.
From violent to vast.
From vulnerable to visible.
From wanderer to wonderful.

From wicked to witness.
From weird to winner.
From yoke to yielding,
From zombie to zealous.

Reflection Corner:

"I wonder what you see Lord, when you walk through the corridors of my heart! I wonder." Well, friend, you know-the eyes of the Lord are upon the righteous and His ears are open unto their prayers. What does He see when He sees us? He does not see as we see. His eyes are more magnificent and deeper than a mere glance. He sees with a deep longing to rescue them that love and believe in Him. He cares for the whole human race and longs for each one to know the unfathomable depths of His splendid grace. May He see the soul for whom He died running to Him with a willingness to be eternally embraced by Him. May He see a sinner saved by grace, singing in appreciation for the free gift of salvation.

26. WHAT YOU SEE

Lord, I wonder what you see
When through the corridors of my mind;
In the cool of my thoughts you walk.

Can I hear you knock?
Are my fingers ready?
My heart palpitating?

Are the doors open and free?
Or am I with my hurts sucked?
Do I come out with you to talk?

Do the windows allow the light?
From heaven's sunshine bright
To penetrate my soul with delight?

What is the sound of the echo?
That pierces through my heart's wall
When your tender voice beckons?

Your admonition I receive.
Lord, you have come my soul to give
The token of your abundant presence;
The gift of a life of eternal essence.

Living for you is not a breath of emptiness;
It is not a thought of purposelessness;
It is the breath of Spirit air upon my soul;
The joy of life in constant helpfulness lived.

Reflection Corner:

Every new day dawns upon us with a mercy package delivered unto us for free. These old sinners saved by grace get new gifts each morning! How awesome. So today, I choose to see the new gifts as they unwrap delicately in my eyes. The gleaming sun rise; the opening petal; the crying baby; the dew upon the grass; the clouds wandering to their known destination; the squirrel in my garden; the ants on the window sill; the winds gently kissing my face-all these He sees. More importantly so, He sees me! He sees my heart and discerns my motives. He is able to assess my thoughts and help me be thoughtfully meditative. Better yet, He sees me through life's pathways. This He does every day. My God has His eyes open. He sees.

27. I WONDER WHAT HE SEES

I admire the changing hues
On the colourful leaves of trees;
The darkening at winter blues;
Yet I wonder what He sees.

The aroma of lavender
My senses engulf.
The morn's still air,
It gladly permeates.

The scent in my sniffing nose lingers
My expectant breath takes it all in;
Oh how I long to catch it with my fingers.
What does He smell when He comes close to me?

The magnificence of colour on autumn leaves,
The perfume of the pretty lilac that breathes;
Adorning my retina with beauty;
Oozing through my breath with gentility.

My fingers caress the gentle petals
Of the pretty roses' blossom.
I stop to wonder the touch immortal,
When I sit upon my Father's bosom.

As I stay connected to the Vine,
I know this tree shall bear good fruit.
As I come to your table and we dine;
I know this work shall have deep roots.

I pray my Father will see
The face of Jesus in me;
And smell the sweet fragrance
Of my character.

I pray the Father's touch
Will douse my thirst to quench,
As upon the Living Water I drink much,
Until by His love I am drenched.

So catch me Lord,
Smelling and soaking your Word;
Be my heart's lifter,
Here and in the hereafter.

Reflection Corner:

Thread. Thread is important to our existence. Our clothes, our furniture, our curtains, our kitchen towels,—are made from thread. One stand alone thread may not be able to accomplish much. One piece of thread cannot make an apron. However, many pieces of thread woven together can produce some of the most beautiful weavings and designs. It is in the weavings of warp and woof that the design of the final pattern of the loom begins to show. Warp and woof must go in the opposite directions for the pattern to be more beautiful. Isn't that how life is? We meet the good and the bad; the warp and the woof. We warp and cross circumstances that make us cry. We also woof and jump on some that make us laugh. The needle of His guidance sews our life's patterns. It is important that we agree to let these intertwine that the loom of our character may be beautiful. Then the Designer's purposes for us will be fulfilled. May it be so with us in the hands of the Master Designer.

28. OF WEAVINGS

I am but a tiny piece of thread,
In the grand quilt my Father has built.
He takes notice of each section He has made,
And ensures the perfect position and fit.

When my Father upon His design looks;
When His gentle hands touch each piece;
His needle of love upon me hooks;
Never a stitch is in vain as He pierces.

The angels in wonder and amazement see
The Grand Artist at work in me.
He prepares my redemption story to tell,
My heart rehearses the song to the "All Hail."

This masterpiece to be on grand display;
This little piece of thread a work complete.
Upon His altar the finished product He lays;
A conqueror I am with no defeat.

Let the devil be entangled in his weaves,
This you know and see.
Cause my heart upon you to believe;
I will not be ensnared like it was at the tree.

Stitch me on my loving Master,
Till your quilting work is done.
Be my character weaving Teacher,
Let me always at your feet learn.

Reflection Corner:

We each have an experience in life that comes to our memory pretty fast. It may have been joyful or painful; nevertheless the memory centre of our nervous system has kept it fresh and brings it out often. Growing up in a Christian environment, I collected lots of memories in childhood. One of those was every night when my Dad would hold us each up on his neck and we would together name and count the stars in the sky. As an adult, I am learning to retrieve such wondrous episodes of true living. I have also gained through life some memories that I wish would remain buried, never to be retrieved. Regardless of the memory bank account slip, you can choose to withdraw and make use of the positive notes. Let the negative ones go to the memory board and be cancelled as bad debt. Be assured that as you pass through the valley of the shadow of death, He is there. You will have trouble, but be of good cheer, because He has overcome. Enjoy the ride, bumps, curves, straight paths and all.

29. MY CHRISTIAN EXPERIENCE

My Christian experience
Is not a luxury cruise.
It is oft beset with sleeplessness
As I run to offer helpfulness
To a soul in need of rest;
To one tossed and tested.

My Christian experience
Is like a lake house;
A place to enjoy His omnipotence;
The need for rest, study and prayer
For a soul worn out by weariness;
For one seeking divine forgiveness.

My Christian experience
Is like an old man by the river;
Waiting for rescue from his helplessness
Before he in this cold catches a fever.
The need to cross over to safety;
The currents are strong and lofty!

My Christian experience
Is like Jesus in a stormy boat.
Evident are His power and presence
Soothing the waves and keeping all afloat;
In my dread of fear I call upon His name.
The boat cannot sink for He paves the shore.

My Christian experience
Is like the rock at sea.
Its surface soothed by the strong waves
That wash away all debris;
A refreshing feeling of calm;
An assurance that I am not alone.

My Christian experience
Is like a boat on a mission;
Daring to cross the raging rivers,
With supplies for the needy on the other side,
A willingness danger to face;
A desire to win one to the eternal race.

My Christian experience
Is like a stone cast at sea;
To the depths my sins are buried;
Never an ugly head to rear;
Cleansed by the crimson stream;
I am now considered an heir.

My Christian experience
Is like being at sea
With my anchor Jesus Christ.
Never do I leave Him at home;
He is always present with us;
My help in time of trouble.

My Christian experience
Is like the deep that veils beneath;
The unseen underground which supplies
All the fresh springs;
Which make the heart glad;
A tap into the eternal fountains.

Reflection Corner:

Oh the looming poverty that is sweeps the streets of our world today. So many are living from hand to mouth each day, while many others could live on their bank accounts for eternity, it seems. Will a day pass by when your eyes do not meet that of another in need? It could be clothes, or food or a home she or he wants! You sense the smile lost in the pile of trouble. You feel helpless to offer a hand. You wonder what sufficiency would satisfy such a soul. Should you dare to extend a hand, you are troubled still with your offering of a pittance of help. Who is your "another?" Have you seen that "another" face that is struggling to cry because the tears are dried up after years under the heat of pain? You see this "another" struggling to walk after months of hunger that have subjected the bones to an emaciation? You wonder what diet plan could revive this organism/this body created by God. Who is your "another?" Please share in one of my "another" experiences in this piece below.

30. SHE IS MY "ANOTHER"

The tattered plastic bag;
Its contents vomited quickly on the highway;
Her feeble fingers drag this possession;
Her thin shoulders shrug,
We judge her drank and in obsession,
As we count the minutes at the end of the day.

Through my windscreen
I squint, her frail body to spot.
Swayed by the wind of night,
Seems like she screams,
She must be caught;
Rescued from this plight.

Cars are roving down in high-speed;
Honking with utter impatience,
Evidently there is an unspoken need,
She must desire some timely ambience.

Her tattered clothes;
The cold seeps through without a fight,
Her bare feet;
I hear her language uncouth,
She is ready for flight,
My heart beats on this street.

Oh, I stop her in her path;
One filled with uncertainty.
I must grab her frail hand
Before another speedy car appears aimlessly.

We echo our voices to each other.
I want to know her agenda
Because I left my house,
In search of one without an earthly father;
An extra bag of food in my car couch
To give another.

She is my "another;"
The other sister that God;
God in His promptings
Has sent me to feed tonight.

She is my "another;"
The other sister that God
Has sent me to,
To bring her clothes.

She is my "another;"
The other sister that God
Has sent me to give a warm hug,
In this cold night.

We get talking,
She has a story,
And one,
Who's willing to listen.

"My boyfriend just kicked me out,"
She weeps.
"Out of where?" I ask,
"Where we stay," She adds.
"Where?" I insist,
"On the street corner,"
She affirms.

"And just now
I have been walking on this road,
Hoping this would be
My last day," She weeps,
"I know God is there,"
"But I told Him,"
"I want to die now!"

"God loves you,
And knows your need,
So He has sent me to you,
To show you that He cares,"
I share.

"What is your name?"
She asks me.
Her voice shaking,
Her eyes teary.
She looks straight into mine
And we realize,
We are sisters
From the same Father.

"I have HIV,"
 She repeats,
As though I never heard her.
"I love you just the way you are."
I look straight into her troubled eyes.

She falls on my shoulder,
Weary and worn from her struggles.
God has come down
To show both of us
That He cares.

My shoulder;
A temporary pillow;
She wets with her flowing tears.
My arms hold her tightly,
I wish I did not have
To let her go,
But I must.

"Where can I meet you tomorrow?"
Hope lingers in me
That this is not the beginning,
Of the end."

She looks at me straight;
Pulls my trembling hands
Towards her lips
And gives me a gentle kiss
And she says, "God bless you."

My husband and I drive home;
I am teary eyed.
Silence dwells with us in the car;
It is evident
Our eyes are locked on her.
She crosses the street
To an unknown bed for the night.

I can only be thankful
That God sent me from His kitchen
To feed this hungry child of His,
But deep within me;
My heart breaks in pieces;
My tears roll like rain drops;
And I wonder how much more
This breaks the heart of God!

I am God's another;
Wandering on the streets of life;
Carrying my burdens;
Dragging them down life's lanes;
Then You stop me, and look at me.

You look at me in the eye;
And you say, "I am here,"
I can heal your broken heart,
Bruised by the malady of sin.

I am here to feed you;
Not with bread that goes stale;
But one baked from heaven's oven;
Coming down to you
With a spiritual spread and aroma;
Meeting your need right where you are;
Bringing you satisfaction beyond compare.

Receive from me.
Look to me and live.
I am here
To wipe away your tears.
I am here;
You can cry on my shoulder.

As you go to sleep,
Know that I will be with you,
To protect you.
As you kiss me goodnight,
I hope you have accepted,
My invitation to guard you,
And my eternal offer.

I will come again to you,
With the kiss of heaven,
My everlasting love to offer;
"Come, abide with me."

My God has spoken,
So, next time I meet my "another,"
I shall not hide myself
From my own flesh.
The question lingers,
"Why didn't I bring you home
With me?"

Reflection Corner:

When we think about armies; when we envision them, we think of wars and insecurities. Armies are important because they offer protection. When an army goes to battle against an enemy, it is not always guaranteed that the army will win. Think about the Israelites and the Egyptians and how the "war" ended. I am on this page not only introducing you to the army that can never lose, but to the Great Commander who always wins. Join Him in the battle and you are sure to conquer. Your enemy will have no choice but to surrender. It is expected of you to listen intently to the Great Commander and follow His instructions. You will be glad you did. Our weapons are not carnal but mighty through God to the pulling down of strongholds. Now, let's go to war.

31. THE ARMY

I belong to an army band.
I am a soldier of the cross.
I have the Great Commander;
In whose presence there is no loss.

The army band has a Commander in Chief;
One that rules not with terrorism;
His battle outcomes know no grief
But on the winning side I remain.

The army band runs to the front;
Fears not the enemy's tactics.
The Commander has no wants;
His crew equipped with His gauntlets.

This army band has weapons;
Not curved by human hands;
Weapons that with great lights beckon;
Eyes look to the territorial Promised Land.

The army band feed from the pot;
Contents brewed by the hand of the Master;
Hungering not for the world's empty roasts;
Satisfied with the Lord's fruitful clusters.

The army band drink from the well,
That the Great Commander makes into a fountain.
The well springs and keeps them well,
And leads them to conquer even mountains.

The army band feeds from pages;
Whence they glean winning strategies,
That no weapon formed against them prospers,
As enemy troops bow down and accept their loss.

The army band waits for the final sound
Of the trumpet that will call forth
All the fighters to come around,
And gather at the foot of the winning One!

Reflection Corner:

Forgetfulness is that plague that we all seem to suffer from. You have been in a situation where you went to a room in your house to pick something, and then when you got there, you forgot completely what it was, and had to go back to where you were to try and remember. I wonder to what extent the advancing of technology is helping us remember important things. We have all these gadgets in our hands, and we plug in our appointments, but still . . . . Well, when we forget to diarize, we are likely to miss out on the "prioritize." The media has not made it easier for us either. We need to remind ourselves consciously who we are, lest the media defines for us our shapes and sizes and slices of fame. Do we then sometimes forget that we are made in His image and likeness? In those instances, what must we do?

32. SOMETIMES I FORGET

Sometimes I forget
That in His image I am created;
And I pump my nature with self;
My ambiance turns to one of stealth.

Sometimes I forget
That His breath is mine for free;
And I begin to wish and regret;
Things not meant for me.

Sometimes I forget
That my eyes are a channel;
To my soul an avenue great;
And I lose the vision of the blessed.

Sometimes I forget
That my auditory nerves must be
Cleaned with the sounds of the Great;
And I miss the echo of His peace and quiet.

Sometimes I forget
That my words must be baked in heaven's oven;
And I feed from earthly mediocre tables;
Missing the abundance of His food that sustains.

Sometimes I forget
To smell the sweet aroma of His presence;
And to His dining chamber I am late;
A child of delayed eloquence.

Sometimes I forget
There is a power at work in my insides;
And I buy into defeat
When I scout the enemy on all sides.

Sometimes I forget;
The future prepared for me is bright;
And I dwell my energies in my present;
Oblivious of His steady guiding light.

Help me to remember;
I am not a child of circumstance;
But a heir of your kingdom; a member;
Guided by your mighty hand of providence.

Reflection Corner:

Jesus is a gentle guest. When He is invited into the heart chamber, He waits to be told where to take His place; yet it is He that created the heart and knows all its places. He is a patient guest; one who will never push for entrance until the willing heart gives over the keys. He is the loving guest who embraces all kinds of people as He finds them at the tables of life. He is the honest guest who speaks the truth in love. When you let Him in and let Him stay, you will be glad you did. The only regret you will have is that you wish you handed Him the keys earlier than you actually did. He comes in to clean up the mess and creates an atmosphere of sweet ambience for the soul. So let Him come and stay; watch how your heart He cleanses!

33. WHEN JESUS COMES TO STAY

The heart is an open house
Where several doors are ajar every moment.
It is the arena where powers
Of light glitter and yet darkness torments.

The heart is like a graveyard
Where carnal bones are buried.
Sometimes the devil's play yard
Where his agenda is hurried.

The heart can be a hospital
Where wounds are evident.
It is the emotion's main capital
Where decisions often turn virulent.

Then Jesus comes to stay,
And the aroma of the chambers change.
He points the door and every way;
And shows us our decisions to manage.

Then Jesus comes to stay
And oils hinges that once with sin rusted.
Windows of blessings are open always;
The light of His presence wanted.

When Jesus comes to stay,
Thoughts are uplifted towards heaven;
Motives are analyzed and weighed;
His presence the whole person gladdens.

When Jesus comes to stay
Hands are released for service.
Feet pave a destination through the right way
And the mind is ready for godly advice.

Let Jesus come in and stay;
Our soul chamber to feed and nourish;
Like a tree by the stream on natural display;
You will grow to the highest and not perish.

Reflection Corner:

Children are good at taking time to find treasures in all places. A vase on the dining table is a treasure to a child who is seeking to drop it down and hear a certain sound. A book is a treasure to a child who can't wait to tear its pages as the parents watch her grow in stages. Treasures are plenty for the eye that cares to catch them and the ear that cares to listen to the sounds they produce. There are treasures at sea, and also within our view. I want to find treasure in God. When He created the seas, He "hid" beautiful treasures there for mankind to discover. As man continues to discover these treasures, we all begin to realize what an unfathomable force of Intelligence we are dealing with; what a wonder! Find the Greatest Treasure; His name is Jesus.

34. FINDING TREASURES

Like a child building sand castles;
Oblivious of life's dangers and hustles;
Like a child seeking treasures buried in sand;
Entertained by the little wet speckles in his hand;

Like a child building castles by the sea shore,
Loving her father's presence and gentle guidance;
Like a child running bare feet not feeling sore;
Unafraid of the oncoming waves in their gentle turbulence;

Like a child building castles at sunset,
Bathing in earth's elegance and kissing the winds;
Like a child mesmerized by the shells at sea and collects;
Counting each piece with diligence as she sings;

So may I be dear Father;
Confident to be safe by your side,
Seeking your face and no other;
Searching for treasures in your Word.

So may I be dear Master;
Following in your guiding footsteps;
For service fitted and moulded;
Anchoring my faith on your constant help.

So may I be dear Lord;
Inviting the wind of your Holy Spirit, O God;
Walking hand in hand with you carrying my load;
Counting my blessings on all life's crossroads.

Reflection Corner:

Sandwiches are tasty, for picnics and for indoor meals. Bread is that one "diet" that seems to work with almost everyone! Sad to say, but not everyone gets a piece or even a slice every day. There are thousands in our world today who still struggle to find bread to eat and others who have more than they can eat. It is a challenging but true paradox indeed. Here is where sharing comes in. There comes a time when you and I ought to choose to share a slice with someone. There must be moments in our days when we feel strongly impressed to carry a slice or more to share with someone on the street with nothing. A sandwich on the front seat is worth it any day. You will not miss someone to eat it. You will meet someone at the traffic light or by the road side. This is your opportunity to open your arms wide and give some help. Truly, as much as life is running fast, there are those who long to know that we care enough to run fast to their rescue.

35. A SANDWICH ON MY FRONT SEAT

My life is running fast!
She's on high speed,
Covering several grounds vast,
Nevertheless a life still in need.

She is up with the sunrise,
Pacing her thoughts to hear
The inner voice of her Father divine;
Then she can go on errands without fear.

She sits her breakfast to feed,
Looking out through her window;
Spots a glimpse of someone in need,
Time to retire away from the indoors.

A sandwich on my front seat,
My companion through the traffic lights,
A hand to stretch with a good deed,
A hungry soul to feed and a countenance lift.

A sandwich on my front seat,
My life's window I roll down,
Scanning the speed of my heart beat,
Wondering if I am a source of hope to a soul cast down.

A sandwich on my front seat,
This aroma someone's need to meet,
Satisfy hunger and share the strength,
When love is stretched to compassionate lengths.

Let not the sandwich go stale and rot,
In the cupboard of your comfortable kitchen;
Unmoved from her storage and spot
In our seemingly well balanced living.

Like a beautiful playing field,
Emptied of kiddie squeaks and joyful noises,
Barren of laughter and dry of giggles,
So is a life that does not heed His guiding voice.

To the highways and byways go;
A sandwich to give to a soul you meet.
You will join in the fight to conquer the foe,
As you go on holy errands through your feet.

Reflection Corner:

We live in Cape Town, and sunshine and winter are awesome here. Yes, it can be very hot or very cold, but we are glad to have life! So I woke up on this morning and was thinking about "myself" and "my comforts." I longed to get back home with my husband to a cup of hot herbal tea by the fireplace. As I drove on the road to his office, my mind was engaged in how warm we would be when we would get back home. God in His mighty power used a simple thought to interrupt my self-raising ego. He brought to my mind the realities of life. He drew my heart to the challenging circumstances of my own sisters and brothers in the cold streets at night with hungry stomachs! He orchestrated a team to join in a blanket distribution drive on this night, and in these precious faces, I saw the Son shining! I am grateful for this opportunity.

36. THE ONLY SUNSHINE I SEE

"The only sunshine I see in my vicinity today,
Is our Red Raspberry leaf tea and our fire place."
How so wrong we often get, how so selfish
When we focus inward and want our needs met!

Let the truth be that the only sunshine I see,
Are the cold faces of my blood bought siblings;
Staring blankly while crouching on the busy streets;
My precious family who call the streets home.

It is the various colours of beautiful skin,
That lack sufficient coverings from the cold.
Yes, it is the hands thundered and rained upon;
Scarred by poverty and lack of food.

It is scanty fingers begging for a slice of bread,
Or a warm drink, and the frail eyes
Filled with redness after insufficient nights
Of sleep on cemented hard beds filthy.

It is the head heavily laid upon the ground;
The pillow; dirt from the shoes of passersby.
The brow that leans upon these hard «beds,»
Wonder about the coming of tomorrow.

It is the runny nose of a small soul called a child,
Hanging loosely on the mother's bent back;
Strapped with a decaying piece of cloth;
Crying for answers that poor mother cannot afford to give.

These are my "sunshine" glowing with the reality
Of the darkness that surrounds us daily;
Awakening my dormant heart with an extra beat;
A beat of compassion to help even one.

These are my "sunshine" illumining my vision
With the reality of a home where them that love Him
 Will never suffer hunger nor thirst, and where now,
 It is possible to wear the garment of righteousness.

These are my "sunshine." This is Jesus on the street!
Cold and hungry, begging for bread and warmth.
«Whatsoever you do to the least of my brethren,
That you do unto Jesus!

He is hungry; I must give Him food.
These are the faces of Jesus;
In Whom alone is the sunshine
And He is the Son that shines.

So, how about hanging out with these brethren,
So we can share the warmth and the fire of God's love?
How about accepting this glimpse of Light,
And going forth to visit with a blanket?

Lord, thank you for a glimpse of your light!
Let me shine for you on the streets of life each day,
May my spiritual weather be always conducive
For my heart and yours to cuddle together always.

Give me a loud heartbeat of compassion,
As we bring you in the form of these brethren,
In to our homes and hearts,
And point our family to our Father in heaven.

Reflection Corner:

We all know that the foundation of a building is critical to its structure and ability to absorb the strong powers of the external elements and remain standing strong. The greatest wonder of the world is not the tallest building (Burj Khalifa)—but you and me—made in the image of God and His likeness; divinely wired to fulfil a particular purpose which He has for each one of us! He desires that even before conception, mothers and fathers will be ready to cement these little souls He gifts us with, "that our sons *may be* as plants grown up in their youth; *that* our daughters *may be* as corner stones, polished *after* the similitude of a palace (Psalm 144:12)

37. THE CEMENT OF THE SOUL

A building is under construction.
The foundation is deep and strong.
The environment is under unction.
But the work is sure to take long.

This building is not made by hands.
The bricks not by trucks transported.
The destination is beyond this land.
The road to the site is not tar-marked.

The walls are not made of cement.
Not manufactured in earthly plants.
Not paid for by human cents.
This soul has a heart that pants!

The cement must be carefully mixed
With the daily sands of life's experiences
That the foundation may be firmly fixed
Upon the eternal Rock in His Omnipresence.

When the cement of this soul is wet;
Be careful what marks remain upon it.
The imprints tend to last!
So leave only that which fits!

It's the soul of a little child.
Pretty yet very impressionable.
I beg you adult don't be wild.
To this tender soul guide perceptibly.

In the tender years of the soul,
May we build upon a foundation solid.
In the impressions we send across,
May none be found sordid.

Let the building come to a completion.
The hands of the parents by God's admonition;
Leaving marks of eternal truths
Upon this soul of cement to soothe.

Reflection Corner:

Reason is often challenged in her position. She is the sister to common sense which has lately become rare to this generation conquered by the media and her visual pursuits of minds and consciences. Reason says, "Think before you do." Emotion says, "as long as it feels right, do." What option are you going for? Would you want to be known as the one who thinks before acting or the one who regrets your actions because you did not take time to think first? Let reason resume her office, for reason and faith are blood sisters, in fact, twins, who enjoy each other's company. Faith is reasonable because it has The Evidence (Jesus Christ)—and though I do not yet see His face, in vision I can behold His beauty. Let reason resume her office.

38. LET REASON RESUME HER OFFICE

Reason has been reporting to work;
Diligently serving and accomplishing her tasks.
Reason's decisions have proved beneficial,
For she listened to instructions from her official.

Reason's performance reviews have proved
That Reason needs to be carefully moved.
A promotion awaits her great achievements
And with that comes awesome entitlements.

Reason employs her common sense.
Her duties are clear and she follows obediently.
Reason has a great mind that never sits on the fence.
Actions she takes and weighs consequences judiciously.

Then one day Reason got fired,
For reasons that Reason never understood.
She was found spiritually inclined
And her workmates saw in this no good.

Emotions took over her place at once.
Disaster did sure suffice.
Reason's office files were deleted hence;
And virtues walked out as in came vice.

Emotions had no room for patience.
She accomplished her work as she felt.
Emotion's attitude made all restless and anxious
And finally someone knelt.

A prayer went forth audibly.
"Let Reason resume her office,
Common sense sees this possibility,"
This prayer must go forth many times.

Let Reason assume her office immediately;
Pending disaster will remain afar
If Reason acts and thinks maturely
And be willing to work with partners sober.

Let Reason assume her office henceforth;
The vision of the life will be realized;
Reason is careful and slow to wrath;
Good tidings will evidently materialize.

Reflection Corner:

Weddings are beautiful ceremonies to attend, and there we meet lots of people. The focus of weddings is not the attendees, but the bride and the groom. Isn't it for the two that we are at the wedding? The groom and bride are often silent, for the man of the hour can't speak much then. Solemn vows are exchanged and great promises are made. Love is in the air and a future is ahead that looks bright and sure. In fact, a Master of Ceremony guides the events of the day. Who is the Man of the hour in your life right now? Do you listen when He says, "I want to guide the events of your day?" My prayer is that you will let Him guide you not only for today but with each passing hour.

39. THE MAN OF THE HOUR

Who is the man of the hour
In my life's daily journey?
Who checks my clock's hour?
Who wakes me up each morning?

Who is the man of the hour?
Who lays food on my table?
I eat the bitter, sweet and sour,
And He says to me He is able.

Who is the man of the hour
In my business transactions?
Who counts me neither rich nor poor
But elevates me to daily sanctification?

Who is the man of the hour?
When I am in need of some rest;
When life's challenges turn sour,
And He says He knows what's best.

Who is the man of the hour?
When my frail body in pain aches;
And before Him I bow,
Asking Him my agony to take.

Who is the man of the hour?
When in my heart confusion reigns;
And I need clarity now;
Then His wisdom pours like rain.

Who is the man of the hour?
When I am at peace.
Upon whose statutes am I a doer?
Jesus the man He is.

The man of the hour
Opens eternal doors;
Keeps away the foes,
Bids me follow!

Reflection Corner:

Boundaries are often clearly marked. Boundaries are important as they show us how far we can go. How beautiful it is that they are marked so that we are not travelling to a "dead end?" Boundaries are important. They saved the life of Job in this conversation between God and Satan. Listen to what they discussed. "And the LORD said unto Satan, Behold, he *is* in thine hand; but save his life." (Jon 2:6). I see that the "but" in this phrase from God made the difference. There was a point to which Satan could not venture. He had boundaries. Job's life was saved. It is beautiful to note that this principle applies to us too. There is a point at which Satan cannot penetrate our core. There is a point at which he cannot open his game to play in our field. God has the boundaries clearly marked. Will you trust Him where you are now?

40. AT THE BOUNDARY

It is at the boundary
That we stop
And choose our decisions.
We look left;
We sure turn right;
Unsure of which way to go,
Nevertheless,
We trust in His might.

At the boundary
We are tagged
By our hearts' desires;
Voices of people
Shouting and alluding,
Join us hence!
Yet we long
To hear the voice;
The one that echoes,
Come with me.

At the boundary
Our mind's in turmoil;
Weighing possibilities
In balances unseen,
In loads unbearable,
Peace often stolen,
Our thoughts rage,
Scavenging for answers,
Often slow to find;
We are our life's managers,
Pieces of stolen peace,
The front yard of our mind littered.

So come to this boundary
Where you find the Hand;
The strong arm of the Master
Holding yours across the boundary;
To a place of stability,
To the arena of clarity,
Where decision making
Is no longer a hassle,
But with His rod
The Shepherd guides
The willing sheep
To the rich pasture.
There the sheep is safe,
Never to be threatened
By the foes all around,
For the watchman at the gate
Has not only the keys
But also knows the enemy tactics;
And when He tells His sheep,
"Be still"
And the sheep obey,
He stills the roars
That cause fear and uncertainty;
And exudes His presence
To comfort the sheep still.
Ultimately, we are safe in His pasture.

Come to the boundary,
Where the hands point
To the right direction;
For the one leading the way
Can never get lost.
He knows the way;
His hands have
The paths paved;
So walk like a soldier brave;
Your commander leads the way,
And the destination is sure.

Reflection Corner:

"If it feels good; do it." We hear a lot about these "cheap" statements that may cause us eternally fatal consequences. Generations of youth are becoming adults, and children are not remaining as children. Every person is growing in age, every day. The question remains, "What other aspects of growth in our lives are we prioritizing? Are we satisfied to be older? Are we content to be known to have lived for long? Or is it enough that I maximize each moment I have by living a life that is transformed?" Conformity to the world is dangerous because the standards of the world are of the devil—who was thrown down here. I want transformation. It is a standard higher, designed by the One who scales us to the utmost of heights.

41. CONFORMED OR TRANSFORMED

In conformity, I do what I like.
In being transformed, God does in me what He desires.

In conformity, my mind dwells on earthly things.
In being transformed, the mind of Christ gives me holy promptings.

In conformity I say "everybody's doing it."
In being transformed I do it because it is right.

In conformity I care less about consequences.
In being transformed, I am keen on His guiding providences.

In conformity, I say yes to please people.
In being transformed my «no» evokes a holy ripple.

In conformity I act first before thinking.
In being transformed I think first before acting.

In conformity my perspective is carnal.
In being transformed my perspective is eternal.

In conformity my concerns are exaggerated.
In being transformed I know I am being chastened.

In conformity I fear to offend people.
In being transformed I fear offending God.

Reflection Corner:

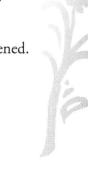

Pride is the malady that affects the nerve endings of our hearts so that any electrical impulses of humility sent to our thoughts are burnt down by the excessively high voltage. This spark interferes in the quiet spaces of others in our surrounding. This causes us to think too highly of ourselves while despising others. It makes us esteem ourselves beyond reality and creates in us a desire to be worshiped, to be someone's "fan." The tentacles of pride are thieves of conscience, stealing away sobriety and replacing in the heart jealousy and covetousness. How shall we tame pride and put it in its rightful place? Can the tentacles be shortened or in fact, cut off completely? My desire is that the tentacles be cut off completely.

42. THE TENTACLES OF PRIDE

The tentacles of pride
Have for so long hanged
Steady, visible and unable to hide,
And human aspirations they have banged.

They sniff at the neighbour's yard,
In search of that object of competition;
Pretending to play innocent on all sides,
Yet eager for undue self elevation.

The eyes of pride manoeuvre and roam,
Rushing to upgrade self above others.
It is never peaceful in its own home,
Imagining there is something better with another.

Pride's ears are attentive to self boosting agenda;
Listening keenly for self defeating strategies;
Marked each day on the dissatisfaction calendar;
Wasting the abundance of one's serving energies.

Now Lord, come forth with your sickle;
Harvest and bury my sour fruits of pride speedily;
They have for so long unknowingly sickened;
Pull out the roots thereof immediately.

Dampen the fertilizer that feeds it;
Let it rot until there is not a root.
Straighten the new branch you plant;
And give me what I need, not want.

Burry pride in the farthest backyard
Where earth's vices find no room to resurrect.
Beat the tentacles yet again hard;
Let there be no negative side effects.

Upon the grave of pride erect an epitome;
Clear view of its everlasting end to all passersby.
Let it not a mound of self glory henceforth form
And let us all say our final and eager goodbyes.

When pride is finally buried,
There's no need for a memorial service.
Henceforth my heart is sacred.
In need of your wisdom and advice.

Let pride be buried;
Let the wreath of arrogance upon its grave rests.
Never can this deadly attitude be sacred;
I am therefore His child in humility at best.

Reflection Corner:

Pity parties are not nice! None of us want to be present in even one. There is neither laughter nor joy in these parties, just cries and moans. What causes them to happen so often? More so, how can it be that a pity party can be sufficient to host one person (the mourner), yet an attraction it remains to the onlooker, and before you know it, the crowd of party members is growing? Well, we create our pity parties when we exaggerate our circumstances and are not appreciative of the present and its gifts. We pick at straws and use them to prick others. I want a party full of joy and exhilaration, but one of temperance and encouragement. Gratitude attracts good company!

43. PICKING AT STRAWS

You have been picking at straws;
The dry foliage of exaggerated trials.
Little wounds magnified as big sores.
Each repetition of your troubles curve you a fall.

Fallen twigs of aimless dissatisfaction,
Symptoms of discontent on the dry leaves of murmur.
A lethargic chorus of complaint and a lack of action.
A shortage of praise to Him in winter and in summer.

Weak footsteps into the immature garden of weeds;
Where nothing grows but stalks of ingratitude.
Look! The devil is planting evil seeds;
Turn back and change your attitude to face His altitude.

Leave the straws the rocks to bury them.
Leave the garden of weeds alone.
Leave the arena of wicked seeds germinating.
Leave the compost and from this garden be gone.

Come now and I will show you a better crop.
Follow me to the garden of unlimited abundance
Where your blissful view can never be robbed
As you harvest the crop of eternal substance.

Let us walk on bright paths paved by the Hand;
The right arm that leads us to the holy table;
A dining after a bumper harvest had;
Let us converse with Him that is more than able.

The leaves of healing are with Him found.
Seeds of deliverance are everywhere scattered.
This garden is built on solid ground.
There we kneel with our fruit at His altar.

Rejoice with me in this newfound Eden
Where there is refreshing fullness and power.
Nothing ever again the soul to burden,
For in our communion our petitions rise to Him every hour.

Reflection Corner:

Can eager voices be heard in prison? Often before we get to prison, the journey has began. This is a different kind of prison, where I find freedom. Read on!

44. EAGER VOICES FROM THE PRISON OF FREEDOM

The earth where I live is a prison.
This is because once a upon a time,
A bright angel lost his garb of humility,
And desired to rise above the stars of God,
And so God threw him down to where I live!

I am not home; I am in a prison,
Yet from this prison house that is temporary,
I have freedom; endless freedom.
I am not surrounded by human walls that can be broken,
But by the Watchman on the Wall of Zion.
There are no bars that keep me away
From interacting with others in my prison cell,
For the barrier of communication that existed
Between God and I has been broken.

It was broken when Jesus was broken on that cross!
I do not lack food, for I eat the Bread of Life day by day.
I thirst not! For my Living Water has never run dry.
I am not naked, I am clothed
With the righteousness of my Cross Bearer.

"My journey with God
Is one of imprisonments and freedom."
What do I really mean?
Why then, does my voice become eager?
Yes, in this life that I live today;
Each day I take a step heavenward
As my Father points the compass towards home.
The trip is not over yet,
But soon shall be.

So what prison then?
It is the prison of an earth,
Torn by pain and agony,
Where we find some rich people very poor
In the knowledge of Christ,
And very poor people rich
In wisdom from above.
Where money is expected to satisfy,
Where innocent children go hungry,
Where the rich eat food unto sickness,
Where the unborn children are murdered,
Where the thief breaks into the hearts of youth,
To lead them into the doorways of drugs and brothels,
Where love is turned to lust and nothing seems to last!

Yet my voice remains eager,
Why?
Because the door of the prison,
Was opened by Love
And it is only a matter of time
And I shall walk through the pearly gates;
But until then, the Good News I bear
Is too good to be whispered.

An eager voice like mine must shout it out!
To the highways and byways,
To the inner city and the church,
To the families and all the living,
That there is Life beyond this prison,
And the most eager Voice did shout already,
"It is finished" on that cruel tree that is now my joy!

Eager voices from the prison of freedom!
Will you join my voice?
I am shouting!
For from this prison, I shall be freed!
I am shouting!
Listen, and then join me!

Reflection Corner:

Is there a factory that produces divine products? Is there a factory that has no waste ? Is there a factory where holiness is manufactured? One where machines don't break down and need no repairs? Yes.

45. THE FACTORY OF DIVINITY

Each morning the sunshine alarm
Wakes me up from my deep slumber!
Before His blood atoning sacrifice,
I come in prayer and praise as I look up.

Then Father beckons me enter
Into His factory of divinity
Where I am the instrument at the centre;
A work sacred, a work of continuity.

He opens the door;
Places me upon His sanctification table;
My character wounds are sore;
Yet the Surgeon's hand is able.

He beats up the rough edges of my conscience,
Sharpens the virtues in His holy presence,
He takes through the fire my attitudes,
I come out sparkling with gratitude.

The water of His love washes my residue;
My demeanour renewed.
The engine of His patience keeps running;
Indeed I am in this race winning.

His forgetfulness of my sin
In the garbage damped in.
No memory banks;
Irretrievable it sinks.

He upgrades me to holy ranks;
He has chastised me and I am spanked
That I may with Him dwell,
And hear the words, "you have done well."

Reflection Corner:

Modelling seems to be an attractive profession to many today. The media is great at capturing scenes that keep the eyes glued on the screen. Thousands of dollars are poured into the modelling industry and many long to be counted among the number. Magazine covers are overpopulated with different models who become "favourites" especially to the youth. Adults are glue to this trend and have "fans." Yet, there is a kind of modelling that lasts forever. It is the modelling of the character of the Greatest Model—the One whose artistic voice brought into reality all that we see today, and some yet unseen. This is the kind of model I want to emulate. He is my "fan."

46. A MODEL

I want to be a model;
Not the kind you see on the screen!
No, my stage is not made of cement or brick;
Neither is it made of pure gold.
There are no flickering lights
That turn heads around,
That keep the people dazed;
There is not a cheering squad,
That applauds what they see.
No, there is not a time-out,
When the event is over;
In fact, there are no hangovers,
No drinks, and no parties,
There are no fashions to be displayed,
No high heels to trick my height.

What is on my stage?
No, I do not have a stage;
I have legions of angels
Watching over me,
That my foot may not slip.
My stage is laid,
Through the merits of the blood;
It is a red stage
Smeared by the sacrificial hand;
Sprinkled upon my heart

That sin may not enter in.
The Son of God is my cheerleader,
The angles are doing the auditions.
I shall not be found wanting,
If by His grace I stick to the guidelines,
For there is no competition,
My Father wants me to win.

He has allowed me another stage;
He grants me two therefore;
One in heaven, another on earth.
The earthly one is made of human hearts,
Soft and tender they are;
No, some are hardened by sin;
And that is why He calls me to join in;
To go and spread the Balm Of Gilead
That healing may spring forth.

As He performs an internal surgery on this stage,
There is no need for halogen lamps;
For the Light from the Son is more than enough,
Guiding my speech, and training my heart;
That I may be a ready vessel to speak a word in time;
A ready hand to offer help for those in need;
A ready mouth to be silent when need be;
Able feet to go where the hearts are found;
A mind after the likeness of Christ;
An attitude raised beyond the altitudes of this world.

Here I am on stage;
Desiring to be a model
Of the Character of Christ my Lord;
And so let there be
No jarring note,
Let there be no human clapping,
Let there be no cheering,
For this work is not my own;
But pour forth in abundance,
A heart of humility;

A look of patience;
A mouthful of praises to You;
A gentleness that attracts;
A kindness that serves;
A peace that quietness turmoil;
And a hope that forever endures.

Reflection Corner:

The oceans are often places of wonder, not only for what is visible, but how far your imagination can take you to "seeing" those creatures and intricate features underneath and invisible. The ocean is indeed one grand feature of His creation whose endings we cannot see. So when I see the ocean, I can't help but think of being soaked in it—as a symbol of His love. Once while at sea, our boat lost its engine power, and there we were, scared of what might have been, but the Love carried us through to safety. May you experience the vastness of His love; more than the grand oceans that He just whispered into existence.

47. SOAKED INSIDE THE OCEAN OF YOUR LOVE

Soaked in the ocean of your love;
The tap of Living Water flows from above;
My whole being herein submerged
By the One splendid Rock of Ages.

Bathe me in your Holy Waters,
That you may present me at your altar;
A creation cleansed from sin;
An ongoing character work within.

Submerge my carnal tendencies;
Conceal them into the depths;
Let my eyes be raised beyond the galaxies;
A child of tender growth on this earth.

Immerse me into your total depths
Till I breathe nothing but your breath.
Surround me thou Rock of Ages,
Till I see your inscription upon my life's pages.

Bury my carnal attitudes;
Out of sight and mind they may be.
Raise me to higher spiritual altitudes;
Your righteousness to clearly see.

In the ocean of your love,
There is no drowning.
You make in my life's waves a cut above;
Allowing me to surrender to your leading.

In the ocean of your love,
The waves roar and beat the shore;
Yet in your presence I have
Much more.

In the ocean of your love,
I find your firm and stable hand.
You remain gentle as a dove,
You pull me away from the sinking sands.

Into the ocean of your love I enter;
A child aware that Father is at the centre
To keep me balanced upon life's billows;
Above the earthly toils and sorrows.

Into the ocean of your love I breathe;
The power supply constant my privilege;
Directions for living you give;
This is pure truth, no human adage.

Into the ocean of your love I calm,
Knowing your hand of mercy strong.
When the mighty waves toward me come,
You respond before long.

In the ocean of your love I listen;
Hearing your voice of sweetness,
As I see the pebbles glisten;
A caricature of my life's pleasantness.

Reflection Corner:

Every day we wake up and get out of doors in order to catch something. We catch the simple sunshine. We want a feel of the cool breeze. The sun's glow upon the mountain should not pass us by. We hear the voice of the neighbours; and eventually we work with our hands so we can enjoy the fruit of our labour. I call it casting nets. The question remains, "Of what use is a net if it is cast on the wrong side? Of what purpose is a net if the fish are dead? If the fisherman is unprepared, is casting a net worth it? If the timing for casting the net is wrong is there hope? Cast your net on the right side and you will make a catch.

48. CAST YOUR NET ON THE RIGHT SIDE

Cast your net on the right side.
The ocean is big; give it a try!
The nets are neither few nor scanty.
The treasures are many.

On that side is the door
Upon which my treasures find release;
For the hand that opens it a jar
Is ready my net to guide beyond the shore.

There are no holes to be found,
But traps for the hungry fish,
Whom The Lord sends me to feed,
As my net He guides to meet a need.

The weight of the net
Is held by the nail pierced hand.
I need not about the future fret,
For He the treasures will find.

And when upon the net I see broken stitches;
I take it to the weaver of life
Who knows how and when to make fixes;
For He remains the life giver.

Fill my net henceforth,
With humanity's needs,
Help me in this spiritual growth,
Upon your word to feed.

Reflection Corner:

The human mind is a precious instrument to be sanctified so as to play in tune with the mind of Christ. The mind can store a lot of information, and at the same time remain very impressionable to the most lucid and also the most incoherent of all things. Thus, the mind can easily get infected with disease that will eventually ruin the life as a whole. We are thus called upon to meditate on proper, pure things and to practice self control. Our hearts are vile, and only with the help of Him who made us, can our diseased minds get healing and restoration. To Him I bring my diseased mind.

49. THIS DISEASED MIND

This diseased mind of mine;
You are at work; my character to refine.
Treasures confined
By you to be released and defined,
For deep within they are hidden,
Yet your power supply bids them be seen.

There have been plagues of worry;
Hurricanes of turmoil;
Tornadoes of defeat;
Winds of doubt;
Storms of anger;
Sunsets of hopelessness;
Rains of despair;
Floods of discouragement;
Thunders of regret;

But now
A renewal process is on
To bring on,
Loads of faith;
Tonnes of peace;
Abundance of victory;
Breezes of quietude;
Sunrises of hope;
Rains of joy;
Floods of blessings;
Thunders of gratitude.

Reflection Corner:

This heart of mine is a building under construction. I need bricks strong to keep the pillars straight. I need the steady hand that never tires to pick me up when my pieces fall, for falling they will when He tells me to look to the Son and I keep my gaze on the gloom. I am under construction, and I am sure that as I remain within His workshop, I will come out a perfect work of art; a willing vessel; to be moulded for His eternal use and purposes. This I cannot do by myself, for I cannot create my own foundation. He does it for me and in me. Meanwhile, brick layer by brick layer I am being constructed. Keep my pieces intact Lord, that I may rise above to see your face.

50. UNDER CONSTRUCTION

My heart is under construction;
I must be rightly positioned.
For a strong work on the foundation;
A work that continues to eternity.

Sometimes a brick or more may fall;
Not because of the Brick Layer's hand.
Sometimes the work may seem slow,
Yet I must with my Builder cooperate now.

His intention is not my downfall;
He uses materials more durable than sand.
Shall I be ready for His nail of commitment?
Piercing through me to keep me committed?

I must be ready for His plumb line of character,
Measuring my character for now and the hereafter.
I must be ready for His spade of sin,
Scooping my filth away and leaving me cleansed within.

I must be ready for His cement of righteousness,
Sealing me perfectly for a ministry of His powerfulness.
I must be ready for His truck of prayer,
Loading me into His presence and away from the slayer.

I must be ready or His roof of grace,
Covering me from sin to focus only upon His face.
I must be ready for His window of sunshine,
Entering upon my heart to keep me guarded with Him to dine.

I must be ready for His door of hope,
Allowing me entry into His Kingdom.
I must not fear when darkness falls,
His ways He will help me to fathom.

Reflection Corner:

After a harvest is gathered, often there is the chaff that remains. With a poor harvest, the chaff is even more. This chaff must be burnt to create room for new growth, and when burnt, the chaff is nothing else but ashes. I like the fact that the chaff creates room for new growth. Even in our lives, we've got chaff! Those things that choke the growth from springing forth, and times come when they must go, or the growth will die. So we welcome the Master Gardener to burn the chaff inside of us. His fire is not meant to burn us up, but to burn the chaff down. His fire is not meant to harm us, but to prune us. Let Him burn the chaff. You will be glad He intervened when He did. Too much chaff makes for an untidy surrounding.

51. BURN THE CHAFF

Father this harvest isn't good.
The wheat has grown with the tares.
There is the chaff, and there is the food;
Call me into your storehouse.

The wheat and the chaff together grow;
The process seems to be slow;
The barn carrying these as one;
But the chaff weighs more than a tonne.

The pieces of wheat that I am;
Growing in your fertile urn
Need pruning consistently,
To mature properly.

Lord, come to this weary garden
Where the tares weigh a burden.
Prune this piece of wheat that I am;
Can I hear your voice of welcome?

Father, please burn the chaff.
Planting it is a task rough.
I need it not for any purpose;
It is pushing the wheat with force.

The residue of the chaff must go.
It is the agenda of the foe
To destroy the wheat;
Your agenda, to grow it fit;

Fit to enter your eternal store;
Where the chaff has room no more;
Where the wheat is in abundance;
Relying on the person of Omnipotence.

Sanctified to eat from your table;
Seated with the One and Only who is able;
Moments of togetherness that last;
With the Omega, the first and the last.

Empowered to exercise in your presence;
The powers that be are of essence;
Adding value to my life's goals;
You remain my one and all.

Reflection Corner:

Daily, we are tested on all fronts, and the temptation is to write "complaints" on the answer sheets instead of gratitude. Oh what a healthier generation we would be if only we scored higher on our gratitude achievement tests every day! This will cause our bodies and minds to function better, excreting hormones at the proper times and enzymes just when needed; each to accomplish the perfect work it was designed to do. We need a happier people, a kinder people, a generation more gracious. Let us score high on this test, on this aptitude. We need hearts like pearls.

52. GRATITUDE APTITUDE

Scoring high on the aptitude-gratitude test;
An achievement in this life a must;
Daily examinations take place;
Grading is in progress minute by minute.
To fit you for the final race.

Crucial are the test results
The Teacher marks each day;
The scores that we surely showcase;
Is your heart like a pearl of great price?
Is it beautiful on display?

A heart like pearls will hear
Sweet tunes of music from above
Where others hear misfortunes;
Enjoy the journey with expectation,
Where others complain about delays.

A heart like pearls will look
Up higher for answers to come down,
Where others look down low, hearts sore;
Forward the journey to continue,
Where others look sideways for a stop sign.

A heart like pearls will see
Opportunities where others see obstacles;
Deliverances where others see defeat,
Hope where others see despair,
Gain where others see pain.

A heart like pearls will shine
With attitudes bright welcoming others to dine;
Where the food of good words are served,
With encouragement in the heart to live,
Where the ambience of joy, traces of defeat unemploy.

A heart like pearls will touch
The untouchable with gentle hands,
Drawing them to the pool of mercy,
Where healing balms never expire,
Releasing them to a life abundant.

Scoring high on the gratitude-aptitude a must;
For it qualifies one for an eternal perspective;
It prepares the human heart to learn to give;
A heart that under all circumstances will trust,
In the guidance of God and His sole directive.

Reflection Corner:

Little walls are dangerous! They are easier to create; easier to build than bigger ones. They take a shorter time to complete and nearly anyone can see beyond them to the next visible object. Children not skilled in climbing walls may think them manageable, and as they attempt the climb, the fall turns out to be painful. Why? There is a deception of strength in the weakness of these walls. Think about Rwanda 20 years ago. Many walls of many homes were broken down so that the perpetrators could accomplish the vile acts. I must confess it is humbling to see pictures of perpetrators and survivors holding hands and enjoying together the abundant food of forgiveness in the absence of loved ones whose death broke the veins of their hearts with bleeding that never ceases! Instead of erecting little walls made of bruised egos, may we like Hezekiah, face the WALL in prayer; meet the Rock who keeps us stable and moves away the pebbles of unforgiveness that litter the pathways of peace in our lives. Lord, save us from little walls that look manageable, yet designed for great falls.

53. LITTLE WALLS

Dangerous are the little walls;
Though small they may seem.
Curiosity they arouse,
The passerby desires to see.

Easy they are to climb,
Much effort not needed;
Yet the knee they may grind,
And cause the body to be wounded.

Are you erecting little walls?
Then prepare for a thunderous fall.
Your rescue may not be nigh;
In pain you may lay and sigh.

Little walls of hatred,
The cement of bitterness fed;
The sun of agony dries it up,
A permanence remains at its top.

Little walls of jealousy,
Paintings of bruised egos;
Bleeding with fearful agony,
Cracks of enmity and foes.

Little walls of bitterness,
The spade of anger feeds it;
Heaps of undesirable vileness,
It is a hard wall with traces of defeat.

Little walls of rage,
Tractors of unforgiveness;
The roughness of the scooped edge;
Loads of expiring tenderness.

Little walls of revenge,
Carried in wheelbarrows old;
Leaking sands of damage,
Depositing bad memories gone cold.

Oh that ye be the wall!
A big and strong one built
By the hand of the Master still;
Straight to remain without a tilt.

Oh that ye be the watchman!
Positioned on eternity's wall,
Souls of men to beckon and win,
No more stories of the fall.

Reflection Corner:

You have probably boarded a flight and sat at the middle seat. No sooner did you take your seat than you sensed some discomfort at least. When you turned to the left, and when you turned to the right, you seemed to have been surrounded by a multitude of peoples! Life sometimes, is just like that. We find ourselves in the middle seat of discomfort, but then the choice remains with us as to what we will choose to focus on as we journey on. We can look through the window and see glimpses of hope. We can believe that the door ahead of us will not remain shut for too long. We can look up to the Light and know that darkness will not engulf us. We will eventually get to our destination. Keep flying. Let not the temporary discomfort in the middle seat bar you from the views above, beside and ahead.

54. THE MIDDLE SEAT

Sometimes life is like being seated
Right in the middle of the middle seat;
Squashed on both sides, truly squeezed;
By circumstances and seeming defeat.

On the middle seat there are fewer options
In movement and dependent on the sides.
Must I ask for permission?
My own feet to find freedom to glide?

Only I know the discomfort
Created while in this position;
Yet I must take plain note
That I have an obligation.

Yes, the middle seat gets tight;
Yet I must learn my roles to play.
I must get up, I need to stand up high;
My desire to speak out, my heart to share.

Get up from life's middle seat and move!
Silence while in here is no great proof!
Speak out to Me what you wish to have;
It won't help in staying aloof.

I arise from my middle seat up high;
No longer in my frail voice a deep sigh;
But energy within to look up high,
For my rescue is right here, very nigh.

My Father knows my middle seat discomforts,
Yet in it He has taught me my desire to speak out.
Pain is never wasted, never for nought;
For in His hands pain never rots but shouts.

Pain shouts as a megaphone,
Our survival skills to hone,
Our temporary blur soon to be gone,
Aren't we nearing home?

This pain that never gets to waste,
But sparks a fire to illumine the darkness,
Burns up rusty hinges and opens gates,
Of storehouses where I count my numberless blessings.

This pain an eternal educator,
In the middle seat a relevant teacher,
At the altar the greatest preacher,
In eternity my forever comforter.

Reflection Corner:

Mountains and altitudes. Isn't that how we calculate the power of a mountain? We measure its altitude!" We know that a mountain cannot change its altitude. It gets its fame with the consistent climbers who push her firm rocks down as they go up, but the mountain stays up high and beautiful. No amount of climbing can turn a mountain into a plain. Regardless of the numbers of climbers, the mountain can never lose its name. The more the climbers; the greater its fame. The higher its altitude the more common its name on the lips of men. We talk of how attitude matters in our daily appointments and disappointments. We discuss during difficult times how our attitude and perspective is of relevance, and then it hits us, "it is hard to try and change our own attitudes!" This is where GRACE steps in and changes us from within. What's your "heartitude" like today? Mountains cannot change their altitudes, but you can change your attitude into a "heartitude" of many virtues. How high have you gone? Are others climbing on you? What's your response? Are you firmly held on to the Rock, or the small pebbles of disgust and complaints are trickling downwards to others with floods of discouragement? Here, you get to choose!

55. "HEARTITUDE"

What's' the measure of your heartitude?
Is it one of love or hatred?
A cut above when pelted?
Of service even when jilted?

What's the scale of your heartitude?
Does it read vengeance when wronged?
Negligence when by standards challenged?
Wickedness when integrity is tested?

What's the weight of your heartitude?
Is it balanced when shaken?
Is it solid when scattered?
Is it found real when imitated?

What's the compass of your heartitude?
Is it steady amidst the strong winds?
Is it to the right direction pointing?
Is it the strength of your heart measuring?

God give me a heartitude of patience
Amidst hatred's outright prevalence;
A heartitude of joy
Despite evil schemes that annoy.

God give me heartitude of peace
Amidst brokenness and pieces;
A heartitude of love
Beyond self to rise above.

My heartitude to beat for your glory;
To gauge my mouth, tell of your story.
My heartitude to be free
From unforgiveness and bitterness.

My heartitude to be filled
With blessedness and sweetness.
My heartitude trained and skilled
To show forth your kindness.

Reflection Corner:

In our technologically advancing space, ideas for business are thrown and scattered to our faces wherever we look. We can see talent everywhere and the skills of entrepreneurship are taught in most institutions today. The challenge is that sometimes we work ourselves to stress because we want to meet deadlines, and when we go on holiday we come back to our email folders breathing at us on high speed. Economies are being driven by the energies of creativity that each one of us has. The driving of economies though, can only be successful if we care to use our talents, time, treasures and body temples diligently. The first point of economy, I must say, is our individual hearts. There is the Greatest Businessman however, whom we can rely on to teach us our trade. He is the one who created the heavens and the earth, and calls us forth to learn from His examples. Welcome to God's business.

56. GOD'S BUSINESS

My God needs no bookstore or farm;
For He is the treasure house of all wisdom;
He is the planter of vineyards and lands;
His business is accomplished by His mighty arm.

His office hours are not restricted,
His angels are active and never affected.
Knock upon His door and register;
As a member in His school to enter.

He works according to the open door policy,
Where none is left out to suffer want.
He opens for anyone who cares to enter in,
To find wisdom for the things they can't.

My God needs no cell phone or landline.
He is accessible all the time.
He created all things and He is fine
Regardless of the man's mastery of the dime.

My God's profit margins are immeasurable,
For He paid the value and the worth for us;
And in our pitiable state of being disabled,
He came to repair our brokenness.

My God never gets weary or tired.
He never gets sick and never gets scarred.
He is the Master mind of miracles and healing;
Only if done in His name and for His glory.

My God's business knows no losses.
He never employs anyone by force,
But the perks and benefits He gives,
Are beyond this world to describe.

My God's business is eternally registered,
For He wants us with Him as conquerors,
And even though we may sin and falter,
He desires our good and still calls us.

Reflection Corner:

The question of destiny and eternity remain prevalent upon every lip. We all ask where we came from and where we are going. The deep desire to know the next step seems to be one that every heart walks. It is important that we find purpose in our being alive, and that each day counts positively towards our accounts of life. From whence have I been cut? Where did I come from? I am certain that I am no work of an evolutionary thought. I am not a mistake of nature; neither am I a happenstance unplanned for. I am not a miscarriage in the womb of earth! You and I were purposed to be born, so let us know that and move on every hour with ingenuity and purpose. Our destination will find us.

57. FROM WHENCE HAVE I BEEN CUT?

Origins never cease to amaze us,
As we go in search
Of our foundations and whereabouts,
And we are eager to find an answer.

To the human race we all belong,
Yet a distinct tune and a song
Is given to each one of us;
So we can't let this echo perchance.

Inherited tendencies we all have,
Those behaviours that have been influenced;
Those traits that our genes crave,
And the passion we have sometimes intense.

Physically we may have similar features,
Yet how distinct our futures;
How unique our characters;
How splendid our individual patterns.

From whence have I been cut?
From which hole have I been dug?
Did I in this play a part?
Oh that I should know and not nag.

The hand that my heart has hewn,
Is His that my soul renews.
The hand that my-self upholds,
Is His whose face I behold.

From whence have I been cut?
From the roots of Jesus Christ,
Found in the garden of His love,
Looking upon myself from above.

Therefore I shall be replanted
In the eternally New Eden,
And there I shall no longer be cut,
But of His throne be a part.

Reflection Corner:

We rejoice when lost items are found; when lost dreams are caught; when lost hopes are rekindled, and when lost energies are revamped. We are delighted when prodigals come home, and when we hold parties to welcome friends back home-they that have been long gone on a journey to another territory. But sometimes in all these rejoicing, we do not realize our "lostness!" We do not see that "we have gone missing!" In our joy for the moment we do not grasp the reality that we have lost precious moments that have thus stolen our niche from us, and we are only screaming in the emptiness of left over hangovers of the joy of another, while we continue to sink deep in our losses. It is time to find our niche and follow it. You were created for a purpose. Pursue it.

58. FINDING YOUR NICHE

Have you found your niche?
Can you try and measure it in inches?
Is it lost in temporariness?
Or it is retrievable in abundance.

Have you found your place?
Can you begin to occupy it with grace?
Is it only a show of your face?
Or it is recognizable in all of your life's phases.

Have you found your slot?
Can you determine the area in life's plots?
Is it only by others caught?
Or it is by you deeply sought.

Have you found your function?
Can you say you have His unction?
Is it only in words mentioned?
Or it is by none else questioned.

Can you catch it?
Do you believe in it?
Can you grasp it?
Or are you imagining it?

Then do not allow another's gift
To cause you a mental itch.
From another's mental yard don't pinch,
But focus on your gift.

Identify the one passion that increases your capacity in great inches.
The one talent that through you makes the life of another rich.
The one zeal that broadens your horizons others to reach.
The one delight that prompts you His goodness to preach.

Reach it.
Catch it.
Preach it.
Use it.

Reflection Corner:

My heart is singing a song whose lyrics say, "He is still working on me, to make me what I ought to be." Indeed that is a truth in each of our lives. Sometimes there are traits we portray or behaviours we exhibit that give others a glimpse of who we really are on the inside. These behaviours showcase our true characters, and sometimes it is already too late to try to hide that which has been exposed. The world tells us to "be yourself," and there is truth in that because everyone else is taken. However, I want to go beyond being myself to beholding Him so I can be changed into His image. I find comfort in the knowledge that He is still working on me. So, bear with this "work in progress." It shall come to pass soon.

59. I AM ME!

I am me! I am me! I am me!
I am "the me" that He is making!
He is still at work in me!
So when you can't stand me;
Kindly face Him.

What ought you to do hence?
Then go down on your knees;
Look intently through the mirror of humility
While in that positioning;
Recognize that you are not a work complete!

Then ask Him with untiring penitence,
To make you "the you" that He wants you to be.
And His gentle omnipresence
Will lead you to look away from me;
Eventually you will fix your gaze on Him.

Cease not each day to come before His face,
For self can show itself in ugly phases.
Upon your heart's gentle pastures self grazes;
It leaves a barren land of thorns and briers,
When you cease to follow His ways.

He is eternal.
I am mortal;
But only for a moment,
The ending of this earthly torment.

All of me He will soon change,
And complete His work in me.
Hence I will be like Him, Immortal,
And we shall see Him as He is!

Reflection Corner:

We have light bulbs of various kinds in our homes and it is often that one needs replacement. So we run to the shop and get the extra one to replace the one blown out. What triggered the blow out? It could be a false circuit, or overuse. It may be the voltage ran too high or even too low. Light bulbs blow out and need replacement. Many times I am like a light bulb that needs replacement. I am blown off by stress and my light stops shining. Sometimes I am overworked and I cower in fear, with irritated emotions that spread darkness in the lives of others. Regardless, my deepest heart desire is to remain that light bulb switched from source, and turned on by the pierced hand; then shall my light never deem, because the source is always plugged. And so I ask: am I a light bearer?

60. AM I A LIGHT BEARER?

Am I a light bearer?
Shining forth streams of brightness?
Penetrating every corner;
Shaming the prevailing darkness?

Am I a light bearer?
His robe of righteousness a consistent wearer?
Beaming joy and gladness in my pathway;
The light of truth to share each day?

Am I a light bearer?
Corners of darkness boldly penetrating?
The life of another to shine fairer,
In the truths of the Light educating?

Am I a light bearer?
Switched on from the heavenly courts?
Brightening the path of the wayfarer;
Stumbling in darkness brought to a halt?

Am I a light bearer?
My torch of obedience always before me?
Scaring the penetrating dark fronts of the slayer;
Shedding truths everlasting, human eyes to see?

Am I a light bearer?
Confident of the path by the Light charted?
Knowing my glorification is nearer;
Darkness of the world playing a part to unburden?

Am I a light bearer?
Focusing upward to my constant source?
Helping others towards the upward look of cheer;
Sin no longer an active force?

Am I a light bearer?
In darkness continuously a glitter?
Others out of bondage and fear;
A welcome to Light's altar?

Reflection Corner:

There is a way in which stench knows how to spread wide and interfere in the spaces of others. When a sewer leaks, even those away from the source are affected. When a sewer leaks, the faces of those inhaling the stench show their evident and visible discomfort. No one wants to be near a sewer, it is uncomfortable. In fact, the big trucks that collect refuse from big sewers have the name "honey sucker." What an irony? Honey is sweet! Sewer is stench! Isn't it clever that they know what emotions a name evokes in the mind? What about spiritual sewerage where vices of the human heart are displayed and the stench is obvious? Love and the eloquence of silence can go a long way in changing the aroma in this cesspool of a world.

61. SPIRITUAL SEWERAGE

Spiritual sewage.
Mortal garbage.
Sin sickness.
Utter wickedness.

In the spiritual sewerage;
There we find mortal carnage;
Death of heart and conscience;
Utter disobedience.

There is unforgiveness;
Where self appraises self;
Active wickedness;
Where none has learnt how to kneel.

There is adultery;
Misuse of God's holy temple;
Leading to lives miserly.
To many, a bad example.

There we find jealousy;
Pain in one heart when another succeeds;
Intentions unclear and lousy;
It runs ahead of itself in speed.

There is an abundance of envy;
Unjustified longings of that which isn't one's own;
Acts of felony;
Intentions coined.

Bitterness in this class is a member;
Coiling itself in the corner of the heart's chamber;
Love outpoured is the healing solution;
Lest bitterness continues its endless aggravation.

Anger is a partner in this process;
Words pour forth from the mouth in curses;
Oh the need to practice the eloquence of silence;
Its maturity and help with no room for malevolence.

Reflection Corner:

Keys are made for a purpose. Keys open doors, and each key is designed to open its own door. Keys are powerful, because they can also lock us out of our own territory when we lose or misplace them. However, the good news is that lost keys can be found, and where they can't be found, another can be made to play the same role the original design did play. Keys are needful. They also lock out danger, when we burglar proof our doors and feel safer than if we let them open, especially during dark hours. Keys are keys, and they serve a purpose, but a key and a door must meet for the purpose to be fulfilled. Forgiveness is one such crucial key.

62. FORGIVENESS IS A KEY

Forgiveness is a key;
That unlocks grudged hearts.
It sets them free from past hurts;
The bondage of discomforts release.

Forgiveness opens doors
That hatred and fear have locked.
It turns positive the hearts of foes,
And removes the negative rebukes.

Forgiveness swings on gentle hinges,
Whose sounds no longer ignite regretful cringes;
But glide through pained heart chambers;
Removing old grudges and lighting up bright ambers.

Forgiveness never bangs its doors to a face;
It receives each lawbreaker with gentle grace;
Beckons each to a greater potential and an embrace;
A new day with hope to face.

Forgiveness' key hole allows for entry
At any time of day or night;
Though it prefers you do not sleep angry,
For the ill passions may cause you to be fiery.

Forgiveness walks the road of humility;
Allows acceptance of another regardless of agony;
Never minds if your sin is one of monotony in its territory;
Calls you to its side in soothing embrace and pity.

Forgiveness flies above the storms of hatred;
Its wings are strong enough to go fast;
To anyone it agrees to be betrothed;
A constant companion whose presence lasts.

Forgiveness never fails
Regardless of how many times you fall.
Its voice is loud to call
Each to repentance and a refreshingly new goal.

Forgiveness reigns,
Whether or not in your heart pain rains.
It lets go of the past and its guilt;
Unto your pain graves not a refill.

Forgiveness always wins,
Regardless of whom the players are at field.
The heart of forgiveness yearns
For you to know that forgiving you can!

At the feet of forgiveness is tender mercy;
That asks you for no subscription fees.
This mercy is free
As you can with your eyes see.

Welcome forgiveness;
A partner and friend;
Compassionate;
Knows no end.

Reflection Corner:

When Jesus was crucified on the cross by the Romans; it was in our place that this crucial sign of our redemption took place. This divine Creator had the power to step down of that cross and send angels to come and wake us up to our call, but He chose to do it Himself. That old rugged cross remains priceless! The risk was high, but His love risked to the point of death, even death on a cross. Remember, dying on a cross was an act totally shunned by everyone at that time. Yet this He did to help us conquer sin; to vindicate His character in the presence of all the living—that He is good! Many times, in this dark world that we live in, self still wants to rise up for first place to catch the limelight. So we pray, "Crucify the flesh in me."

63. CRUCIFY THE FLESH IN ME

Crucify the flesh in me.
Nail it hard with the hand that was pierced
On that cross; turn my head that your face I may see
And believe that I am blessed and not cursed.

Crucify the flesh within.
My heart in you to conquer therein;
Tagging my feet tethered closer to yours,
Each thought and motive beneficial each hour.

Crucify the fleshly lusts visible.
May I recognize your power invincible;
Pulling my heart strings to your heavens,
As each day I feed on your Word given.

Crucify the fleshly motives.
The guile of my heart's thieves;
Stealing away my joy of redemption;
Oh that I accept your gift of free salvation.

Crucify my earthly desires;
My heart and mind be heavenward wired;
Thoughts that glorify your kingdom;
As you prepare me for that eternal home.

Crucify the flesh in me;
Raise me to a life everlasting,
For in dying with Thee,
I live unto eternity.

Reflection Corner:

Open doors and closed doors. They each serve a purpose. When opened, there is the opportunity for entry and exit. Closed? None can dare enter in. Temptation lurks and lingers near us all the time, and when the doors are open, they are likely to walk in without permission. Satan is the originator of temptation when he said to Eve in the Garden of Eden, "Thou shall surely not die." His ways are known to us for we are not left unaware of his tactics. Since we know that he has no good agenda in store since the foundation of the world, how much more ought we to beware and stay vigilant? May God help us to shut the door to temptation using His own keys.

64. SHUT THE DOOR TO TEMPTATION

Shut the door to temptation with "It is written."
Let it be the key that closes the door on Satan's face;
His winds are meant your soul to threaten,
But the Mighty Eye of God upon you a holy gaze.

Bang that door with energy divine,
Your countenance to remain sublime.
Tell him your Master has the key,
And not only that, He also paid the entire fee.

Care not the sound of that door's hinges.
Hasn't your cheerleader guided you with his finger?
Make the bang ever so loud;
You will make God's heart proud.

When the lock and key finally meet,
Stay seated at your Master's feet;
The enemy a perpetual defeat,
Your weapons of courage God alone creates.

Open the door to the Master always,
For the wiles of the foe
You cannot keep alone at bay.
A tempter he is and his agenda known.

Open the door to the Master and let Him in;
Let Him feed you with abundance and holiness divine,
Then when Satan tries to break through,
He will find that your God has guarded you.

Reflection Corner:

Are you a victim or a victor? Check out this scale and determine how you measure up. Ultimately, in the great controversy the Victor is Jesus Christ, the victim is Satan. It therefore matters what we feed our minds; what we say and what we see, so that we can grow to be victorious.

65. VICTIMIZED OR VICTORIOUS

What food are you feeding your mind today?

Victimized says, "People are hurting me,"
Victorious says, "We fight not against flesh and blood."

Victimized says, "My circumstances are overwhelming,"
Victorious says, "The God of all circumstances is winning."

Victimized says, "I don't need people,"
Victorious says, "Good and bad traits in people help me grow."

Victimized says, "You don't understand my situation,"
Victorious says, "God understands and has the solution."

Victimized says, "This is too much for me to bear,"
Victorious says, "I can lay my burdens upon the God who cares."

Victimized says, "Leave me alone,"
Victorious says, "With God I have won."

Victimized says, "Never again!"
Victorious says, "The Cross is my gain!"

Victimized says, "Tit for tat is a fair game,"
Victorious says, "I shall go forth in Jesus' name."

Victimized says, "Don't worry about me, I can handle,"
Victorious says, "I need the prayers of those I love to handle."

Victimized says, "This is my fate,"
Victorious says, "I live by faith."

Victimized sees the size of the problem.
Victorious sees the vastness of God's love emblem.

Victimized sees human interference.
Victorious sees God's providences.

Victimized revenges.
Victorious lets God avenge.

Victimized envisions the pending catastrophe.
Victorious wins battles on bended knees.

Victimized uses human ammunition.
Victorious uses God's weapons of admonition.

Victimized looks inward.
Victorious looks upward.

Reflection Corner:

A distinct sound is one that is clearly heard, and cannot be mistaken for another. We enjoy walks in the forests and hiking on mountains. I know that even the trees of the forest whistle and the crickets sing. I enjoy it when the birds echo forth their joyful noises and the toads by the river sing aloud after a shower of rain. What sound of distinction are you reverberating so that through His righteousness you may wear a crown? Is your whistle loud enough to call someone forth from the ways of danger? Is your trumpet voluble enough to invite someone to the table where you have learnt to dine with the Master? Sing your tune! Sing the tune that has been wired within you as you remain firm and immovable where God has planted you. Produce a distinct sound that will bring together many vocalists to join the eternal choir of the redeemed.

66. A DISTINCT SOUND

A distinct sound I vividly hear,
Yet not from the trees that appear.
I only need to walk near
And a solemn sound falls in my ear.

A few confident paces I go ahead;
I stop and then turn my gracious head;
The trees are still widely spread
Yet did the sound finally go to bed?

Again I walk and hear the sound clear.
Indeed I need not fear,
Though this may sound queer;
The sound is only audible in certain spheres.

I stop to think upon my Christian tree;
What "certain" sounds do I produce
When passersby come by near me?
Do they find me of any use?

Is my sound sweet to the ear that listens?
Do the onlookers see my leaves of character glisten?
Are my branches upon the Vine fastened?
Does my sound the appearing of the Vine hasten?

Lord, help my Christian tree;
A sound of warning to shut aloud
That we whom you priced at Calvary,
Will remember that eternity you can afford.

May my Christian tree be distinctly different;
Producing fruit that leads to a life of reverence
To you and your holy precepts;
Sanctified with divine realities and perceptions.

Let the passersby stop by and listen.
Their spirits with your love quicken,
To walk in obedience and faith,
Towards that golden everlasting gate.

Reflection Corner:

Bridges are crucial for passages from one destination to another. They are needful in instances where there is an evident need for a passage way. Bridges are also built when the natural land and sea creations of God meet. When sin separated us from God's original plan for our eternal life with Him, God constructed a bridge—the cross of Jesus. This cross connects God's throne to the human heart, as in Christ the humanity of man is clothed with the righteousness of Jesus Christ. It is therefore our joy, that Jesus has shown us the example, and today, in our troubled world we can construct bridges to make life easier and better for one another. May He remain our anchor as our bridge stands firm to the end, so that as we stand at the sea of our challenges, we can still see the Land of Promise.

67. CONSTRUCT A BRIDGE

Construct a bridge of love;
That the hearts filled with hatred
May know the heart of Him above;
A friend whose gardens spiritually feed.

Construct a bridge of joy;
Let the sad faces find freedom
To express the reality of their attitudes coy;
And be prepared for the eternal kingdom.

Construct a bridge of peace;
Let the troubled soul pass through;
Burdens to carry and bring to Thee
He who takes them upon His cross a new.

Construct a bridge of hope;
The downtrodden to find encouragement;
Saved from Satan's desire to elope
And welcomed to God's dome of blessedness.

Construct a bridge of patience;
The weary soul to wait upon with no complaint.
Guide the feet of the slow with diligence,
Till the destination we arrive all jubilant.

Construct a bridge of kindness;
A timely word to speak,
A gentle, helping hand to extend
As together we climb character's peak.

Reflection Corner:

A human body runs on oxygen supplied by the blood; lack of which may cause many more disturbing health challenges. Anaemia is one of those challenges. It is known to be a dangerous state for the human body to be in. We depend on oxygen to be alive, and a deficiency of that in the body lends it to suffocation for the cells that need it most. Surely, there can be no life without oxygen, so God in His mercy has granted us an abundant supply of this oxygen to make life possible. It is thus the same for the Christian. The graces and virtues imparted to us from Christ enable us to live a life that pleases Him. What makes for an anaemic Christian? One who lacks the divine supplies to keep the Christian heart beating? How can we prevent this malady from attacking the recesses of our minds and hearts? So I pause to ask myself what kind of a Christian I am. I hope you do the same.

68. THE ANAEMIC CHRISTIAN

Am I an anaemic Christian?
The oxygen life giving supply lacking;
Weak in faith;
His word unable to absorb?

What are the nutrients of my spiritual diet?
Is the variety abundant?
Or I am resorting to temporary supplements;
And forsaking the energy giving food of the Lord?

How red is the blood supply?
Have I received it enough from His abundance?
Can He hear my heart's cry?
When I cannot stand long due to weakness?

Is the air of the Holy Spirit sufficient?
Can my lung of grace keep me breathing?
Indeed for myself and out unto others,
Filling life's spaces and moments with rejuvenation?

Cure my anaemia with your tablets of love;
Let me swallow the pill of faith each day;
Your Son's rays shining from above;
To warm my blood of faith with what you say.

Give me an abundant supply of spiritual energy;
To reach out to layman and clergy;
Eyes filled with love and a yearning
To bring the weak to your haven transforming.

Breathe on me the breath of God;
Fill my lungs with the power of your outreach;
That I may hold a hand weak and cold,
With the chord of love and a timely word preach.

Reflection Corner:

Chains cannot be chains unless one is connected to the other. A Christian is like a link in the chain of life, bringing hope and encouragement to weaker chains. We all get to that point where our chain of patience is weakened; where our chain of joy gets saddened, and our chain of peace crashes to pieces. Aren't we so glad still, that there is already the Link that connects heaven and earth? For our own safety, we must remain connected to this link so that we may pass the currents to others on the journey through life. May your link remain strong each day as you connect to the Link that can never break.

69. A LINK IN THE CHAIN

Am I a link in the chain?
Connecting the human with the divine;
Revealing to hearts the eternal gain;
Received when with Him we choose to dine?

Am I a link in the chain?
Prayers ascending to the Father's throne;
Souls for whom He died to remain;
On His side for eternity and more?

Am I a link in the chain?
Songs of encouragement sing;
Soothing hearts that are in pain;
Balm of Gilead remaining my King?

Am I a link in the chain?
Offering a presence and a comfort;
To one lonely and weary;
Show them the Lord's haven of rest?

Am I a link in the chain?
Encouraging others the narrow way walk;
His Holy Word daily to crave;
In Jesus and of Him we share and talk?

Am I a link in the chain?
Supplying help from the Master's store;
Sharing beams of life and His promises claim;
Shining unto the eternal day Him to adore?

Am I a link in the chain?
Hope to share and love to spread;
Cheer to weave on lips chained;
Remain connected to the eternal thread?

Am I a link in the chain?
Eternity in my immediate view;
Connected I stay close to the King;
Strengthened heavenward to go?

Reflection Corner:

A candle is only beneficial and functional when its flame stays on. I know of a famous song with the following lyrics; "here is a candle in every soul, some brightly burning, some dark and cold." The song encourages each one to carry our candle and run to the darkness. What makes for a dark and cold candle? Its flame is off. However, I know the One who can keep the flame on. He knows how to clip off the rough edges of our wicks so that the flame glows brighter. In fact, there is no trace of smoke! Let your candle shine bright day and night, and you and the ones who enjoy the warmth will wear a crown and see the face of the Light.

70. THE CANDLE ON MY HAND

I held the candle on my hand.
I watched the flame flicker.
Each drop of wax fell gently to the ground,
The candle length did get shorter.

My thoughts flowed in wonder
As life lessons I pondered.
Yes the candle stick did get shorter
But did its flame get any weaker?

Bright it beamed the whole time.
My clock did tick and chime.
Then finally its voice it raised,
As upon it I maintained a steady gaze.

Oh Christian, with each passing day,
The clock of your day flickers and life shortens;
But like the candle, are you lighting the way
In a world of darkness with lots of torment?

While the wax was hot amidst the flame,
Did your life burn bright with holiness?
The knowledge of Him never to you a shame?
But a life of purposefulness and righteousness?

Will your wax be just another statistic?
Another happenstance that befalls humanity?
Or will it be a season fantastic,
When all recall your works and life joyfully?

When your wax finally to the ground falls;
Let the evidence be of a life that was lived.
What content will the echoes of the voices recall?
Of what purpose did you live?

As the wicks of your seconds continually burn;
Oh how I pray precious lessons you garner.
Shine a light, whose brightness never weakens;
Unto others light up the way to the heavens.

The Light of the World urges
All to be a candle;
Shining His light and silencing dirges;
Glittering with peace life's burdens.

He makes and repairs the wick,
Strengthens it with His holy oil,
To keep a flame even the weak,
As we grow in His righteous soil.

He calls upon the entire world a candle to be;
Showing the way to the source
Where brightly beams continually
Flicker through days and hours.

Let His wax of healing cover your wounds;
Let His brightness go beyond your neighbourhood;
Ablaze all the hearts with His light of love;
Sparkling all hearts with fire from above.

Let His flame burn the dross
That wants to leave a stain on the cross;
For indeed He has paid the prize;
His cross of Calvary is more than enough.

Carry your candle wherever you go.
Flash your heart and that of others too.
Glow brighter from now to the end.
Each you meet to be an eternal friend.

Reflection Corner:

High walls and electric fences. Barricaded gates and security guards. Alarm systems and angry faces. These seem to be the sign posts at the gates of most of our homes in this generation especially in the cities. These gadgets call for high voltage to keep the enemy at bay. Yet there is a kind of voltage that is attractive. It is the voltage of gratitude; and it can come in large doses without any negative side effects. The currents can stay on the live wire of praise without causing any emotional electrocution. Welcome the voltage of gratitude in whatever amounts and you will be attractive to both the sad and the joyful.

71. THE VOLTAGE OF GRATITUDE

What is the voltage of your gratitude?
Is it in the watts and wants of attitude?
Or the killer-watts of complaints
Registered in your heart's domain?

What is the current of your attitude?
Is it a thing current and present?
Or a story of careless resentment
Known by multitudes?

What is the weight of your gratitude?
Has it been strengthened by your heart's fortitude,
Or weakened by life's tipping scales
Covered in agony's veil?

A heart of gratitude is a must.
To the Christian this attitude to wear;
Not only of the things past,
But regardless of your present tears.

A heart of gratitude is the barometer;
Measuring the temperature of the Christian at the altar;
Coming before God to bow down in joy and peace;
Unobstructed by whatever else is breaking to pieces.

A heart of gratitude is the gauge;
Filling the Christian's heart wallet at any age;
A thankful heart to the Desire of Ages;
As He joyfully writes our stories on life's pages.

A heart of gratitude is the blessing counter;
Numbering the gifts and sorrows at once;
Thankful for all of life's detours and contours;
Believing in the God of second chances.

Reflection Corner:

However busy life seems to be with today's dual career families, mothering remains an honourable calling to women. A child's tender years are most crucial to his or her growth; therefore being a mother is a full time sacred assignment. The wellness and safety of the child entangle and consume the thoughts of the mother at all times. This responsibility cannot be solely left to the hands of caretakers. Indeed children are a gift from God, but a mother who loves God and directs that child to God is imparting even a greater and more perfect education to the child. I pray that you will let Jesus teach you how to be a mother after God's own heart; that you may draw the hearts of your children towards the heart of God. May your heart remain close to His always; that your children will be attracted to His gentleness and love.

72. ON MOTHER'S KNEES

On mother's knees;
There she makes her plea.
Her desire is clear;
Often communicated in tears.

On mother's knees
She weeps.
Her heart in crisis;
She comes with her sobbing cries.

Mothering her role.
This a spiritual call.
To help her when wounded.
To give her the care needed.

Mothering her job.
Sometimes she too sobs.
Yet her work must continue;
This soul with His spirit imbue.

Mothering her work;
A great and mighty task.
Mould this soul for life now;
Help with courage and no cowardice.

Mothering her times;
Moments given to nurture.
The clock will chime;
Ahead is the future.

Mothering her opportunity.
Tell this soul of life eternal.
Prepare the heart to fight agonies.
Education formal and informal.

Mothering her responsibility.
Providing for wants and needs.
Careful to groom these abilities.
Gently pluck out the visible weed.

Mothering for God's purposes,
Praying without ceasing.
Wisdom in full measure.
To the mother who listens to Him.

Reflection Corner:

With the passing of time and history, adornment has seen many faces. In the olden days, most people preferred simple long gowns. My pictures of Jesus when I was a child don't seem to have changed much! I still see Him as the simple man who had a big chair in heaven, but came down to earth to take our place and sit with us on the ground. He was adorned in sack cloth—in humility. This cloth of humility is one that looks beautiful on anyone if properly adorned. When the garb of humility is worn upon our hearts, respect for one another is esteemed highly and we place ourselves in the right place by having a right estimate of ourselves. Don the sack cloth of humility and the moths of pride and arrogance will not find a fitting lace for their itchy dwelling. Humility is awesome!

73. DON THE SACKCLOTH

Don the sackcloth.
Bring it back into style.
Let it not be eaten by the moth.
Remove it from your wardrobe pile.

This sackcloth with buttonholes
Of humility to adorn each hole;
Gentle treatment of the nearby wearer;
Touching each with love and care.

This sackcloth woven with simple thread;
The hand of the weaver strong and steadfast.
It is free and can be cast abroad;
The weaver a servant and a friend.

The colours of the sackcloth not many;
Just the plain simple colour of humility;
The greatest thread to weave in your character;
The stitches to remain in place today and hereafter.

The needle that passes each hole a work of repair;
Let it prick the proud heart and set it free;
Free from the bondages of earth's materials and fairs;
A hand ready to serve and a heart that gives.

The sackcloth must be washed in the blood
Of the Lamb slain from the foundation of the world.
All stains fall off in chorus and jubilation;
New cloth woven in my heart through salvation.

Goodbye moth, you have no room on this cloth;
For the price has been paid and I am bought.
This treasure in jars of clay;
Warmed under the Sun of righteousness each day.

Here is my sackcloth Lord.
Take it and make it clean and pure.
Weave my heart with cords of your Word;
A humble servant to all far and near.

Reflection Corner:

A traitor is a liar—disloyal; defector—one who has been on your side then absconds. A traitor does not give the correct statement of a circumstance as it were. Traitors are more skilled in causing downfalls. Traitors do not appreciate the uprising of one from lowliness to abundance. Here is breaking news: that each and every one of us has a traitor within. Traitors can be visible or invisible. Traitors of blindness cause our vision to be clogged and we run short of the purposes for which God made us. Traitors of anxiety echo loud the voice of "*I can't*" and are always begging for us to prove ourselves. Yes, self is the culprit. We need to not only search our own hearts but seek His hand of rescue to help us lest we be consumed.

74. TRAITORS WITHIN

There's a traitor within
Each heart and soul of mankind.
This traitor garbed in sin;
The spiritual vision to blind.

The traitor is a great pretender.
Friendship ties it fastens.
You will not think him an offender;
Yet its wile tactics it hastens.

This traitor is tricky and witty;
Covers up its true motive;
Underneath are components filthy;
Its work remains active.

The traitor of self to domineer;
Wanting my ways above all else.
The spirit within me disappears.
My heart eternally fails.

This traitor of self to the cross I send;
I need the Lord's help, my knees I bend.
Conquer the traitor in me that breathes;
Selfish motives in my heart it bequeaths.

The traitor of selfishness to abase;
It must leave my heart speedily.
I am on the winning race.
There must be no room for this activity.

Traitor of pride a show off of ego;
Everywhere it follows on as I go.
Hit with your armour this daring evil.
Uproot its roots that are planted by the devil.

Traitor of unforgiveness in my heart aches.
Scoop this snare far from me my Maker.
Search my heart's chambers this enemy to chase.
Be my soul's undertaker.

Traitor of covetousness likes to linger.
Unsatisfied it remains, always pointing a finger.
Egoistic seeds grow in my character garden;
Hoarding for self becomes a burden.

Traitor of sin;
You are the enemy within.
Lord, I am under your judgment.
I confess I need treatment.

Treat me with your capsule of love,
As I swallow with waters from above.
Inject me with your syringe of grace.
Heal my feet and bring me to finish the race.

Pierce my soul with your righteousness.
Smear my heart with your balm of sanctification.
Let my medicine be wrought in thee.
Wipe my wounds with your nail pierced hands now free.

Restore unto me your preventive measures;
Dominion over sin my greatest treasure!
More than a conqueror;
A fighter and a mighty warrior.

Reflection Corner:

Cancers, fibroids, name them. Tumours are plaguing this generation; and in various forms the medical professionals have coined names for various ones. Some are malignant while some are classified as benign. Thanks to modern science but; some of the most fatal tumours are those that the doctor's eyes cannot see; neither can their precise and modern equipment detect. Yet these tumours remain in full view of the eyes of the Great Physician. These tumours cannot be removed by the most modern surgeon's scalpel. They cannot be diagnosed under the most recent medical equipment; neither can the symptoms be outlined in full. One such fatal tumour is unforgiveness (failure to forgive). When it lodges itself in the chamber of the heart, it stops the flow of the blood supply of life to the mind! It loathes people and holds grudges in its veins. Watch out for this fatal tumour! The cross is the only scalpel perfect for this job.

75. THE TUMOUR OF UNFORGIVENESS

The tumour of unforgiveness;
A tumour vile and virulent;
Is feeding on the life veins of many,
Causing untold stories of agony.

This tumour blocks the ceaseless pathways of breath.
An ugly aroma to send through life's veins.
A diseased body, a sick heart, a decaying mind.
Helplessness crawls near to such a one to bind.

Give your heart to the Great Physician;
Let His knife of peace cut up the rotting layer;
His aroma will replace your heart filled with stench
As He heals your wound and your arm He clenches.

Give this tumour to the Balm of Gilead.
Let His abundant supply of blood the wound clean;
Your breath to give life, your heart a song;
Yes, an added number to His golden throng.

Give this pain away to the heart of Jesus.
His pierced hand to soothe every nerve and sinew.
A work of restoration He completes in us;
Your heart with energy to beat a new.

Give this baggage to His strong shoulder;
He is more than able to carry you through;
He will clean the dirty chambers and folders;
Then He Himself will sit there and guide you.

Give this agony to the comforts of His Spirit;
His feet will walk toward you, your mind to lift;
A new perspective to have of life in Him;
Your clean breath with song and praise to fill.

Give this monster to the Ultimate Conqueror;
One who has never lost any battle.
He will fight for you with weapons stronger;
Your name to hang on heaven's wall articles.

Give this distraction to the Pathfinder;
His hand to direct you to the All-Powerful source;
Your destination will remain sure,
Your heart and body to fill with vital force.

Reflection Corner:

A house burning down with belongings inside; a forest blazed away by the start of one little cigar butt; a prison cell burning down with inmates! These are unwanted fires. A fire with a destructive purpose is one that no one wishes for. Fires that are unwanted are hazardous! Speed is needed to extinguish those kinds of fires to avoid excessive damage. On the other hand, a fire with a purpose is a welcome delight. A fireplace at home during winter; a bonfire under the star lit night; a three stove fire for cooking food at a camp out. These are all good. The Bible uses the symbol of fire to signify the Holy Spirit. Without the Holy Spirit's fire burning deep inside of us, we are likely to be the Laodicea.

76. LIGHTING A FIRE AT LAODICEA

The ground in Laodicea
Is wet and mouldy.
Passersby walk, slip
And fall on this path muddy.

The rains of blindness
Have blurred the vision.
The winds of wickedness
Have altered the mission.

The nakedness
Of unrighteousness
Has whipped the heart
With the cold winds of sin.

The wretchedness
Of lifelessness
Has bitten away
The joy of service.

The poverty
Of lawlessness
Has increased measures
Of slackness to duty.

The want for faithfulness
Has imprisoned
The storehouses where
Pure love once dwelt.

There's need for a fire,
That will dry up the mould;
Prepare ready ground for moments
To stand tall amidst toxicity.

A fire that burns the chaff;
Eyes to open to the reality
Of the urgency of our mission;
A mission that must be pursued.

A fire that would warm the threads
Of righteousness.
Clothes of purity to design;
A burning that echoes malleability.

The chaff of sin to quickly blow away;
Dull minds must now be warned
And awakened to fruitfulness
In works and in righteousness.

Sin must be left in pale ashes;
Lovelessness must be resurrected
From her grave of apathy and carelessness
To heights above and beyond to eternity.

Obedience to the Lawgiver
Must be the ticket to riches;
Riches found only in obedience
And not in manmade dockets.

These riches are calculated
Not by humanistic theories
That justify human behaviour
And grandiose carnality.

The riches are calculated
And measured in divine ideals
In the sacred scales
Of heaven's purity.

This fire must burn up
Our comfort zones and send us
Running to the rescue of the perishing,
Reducing to ashes our manmade comforts.

This fire must shape the metals
Of eternal characters
That lead us to build Ebenezer points
Of solace and service to one another.

Reflection Corner:

Snails are slow, and that is just how they move around-slowly. We can learn great lessons from snails. They have a purpose for carrying their "homes" on their backs—it is their protection—where their soft tissues and internal organs are sheltered. For us humans, despite accessibility to good road networks and transportation in most parts of the world, there still remain loads that we must carry on our own. The weight of a heart cannot be weighed on a machine. It comprehends it not! Could we be faster paced if we let go of our burdens and our cares? Could our speed increase if we focus on accomplishing the purpose for which we are here? Slow paced in today's world with Jesus at the door may not be a very good option at all. Let us not run ahead of the race, but run the race that has been set before us, that we may come forth as more than conquerors.

77. THE SNAIL CLASSROOM

Are you carrying your burdens around?
Forgetting to see His grace that abounds?
Is your life pace at snail speed?
All your troubles your heart to feed?

Watch the snail on its errand;
Slowed down by its burden grand;
Its destination a way far off;
Danger on its trail if it won't back off.

Like the snail we often behave;
Our burdens to protect in our enclaves;
Weighed down by ugly weights;
Or can I learn lessons on how to wait?

Oh that I may learn of Thee;
Wisdom to truly see from nature;
From the snail to know my boundaries
And that your capacity can bear my agonies.

The snail along its pathway slow;
May I learn the enemy of progress
And onward in life as I go;
In you to find the mighty fortress.

Lord, carry my burdens for me;
On my own the future I cannot see.
These burdens tend to weigh on my vision
And I am blinded from your real mission.

May I not be prey to circumstances;
But pray for your holy providences;
That as I journey through life's phases,
My intentionality is to see your holy face.

Reflection Corner:

Fashion designers never seem to run out of ideas. Magazine covers and television channels are dedicated to fashion and her strong character of persuasion for many onlookers. The human eye never seems to have enough to look at! In a world where pictures can be sent from one continent to another in a matter of minutes, pictures are prevalent and very important in communication today. What if fashion was designed and worn on the inside? It is possible our human eyes would not be able to spot it. However, there is a kind of fashion work that I know. These are neither done by human hands nor are the designs temporary and changing like what we see in the media. This Designer starts His work on the inside, and the effects are obviously seen on the outside. What a wonderful design He creates in each client willing to be fashioned by Him!

78. FASHIONED

I see the outlaid pattern visible.
Fashioned after the Creator's similitude.
His work of art none to fully comprehend;
His creative artistic genius never to suspend.

This fashion unlike the human design
Begins a work in the interior.
Chambers of the heart toward His tools incline,
A work on the outside too of great effect.

A mind clear;
A heart pure
A smile
That others positively affect.

The tools of His trade may seem rough
Yet His work is never left in half.
In the privacy of your heart a part,
Where His dwelling and presence last.

Fashion me after your likeness;
Clothe me with your glitter of righteousness.
May the thread that runs from your loom
In to my heart be woven; into my soul hewn.

Spotlessly clean me and keep me stable;
My character spots touched by your thimble
As this piece of your work,
You lay upon your everlasting table.

Stitch my brokenness with your needle of perfection;
Weave in me a pattern of your reflection;
The colours hewn to show forth your majesty;
A complete work of holy tapestry.

Reflection Corner:

Recently we had a beautiful opportunity to visit a potter's workshop. We found the potter busy with his designs that birthed many stunning pots of various shapes and sizes. As we watched him, one lesson became clear. The pots were obedient! With each attempt to shape the pot according to his desire, the clay responded. We were mesmerized at how within a short time, a blob of clay was transformed into a beautiful work of art, and customers came rushing to buy what they liked. Jesus is the potter and we are the clay. Often times we are cracked pots, but aren't we so glad that the Potter wants to fix us back together again? Are we easy to mould, shape and be formed into His likeness?

79. LESSONS FROM THE POTTER'S HOUSE

The work begins with dirty clay;
Filled with clods of sand and pebbles;
Covered in murky waters each day;
A work He does with His hands able.

The Potter is diligent at His task;
He has a picture in His mind
Of the outcome of His final product;
And He touches the clay with gentle hands.

He weaves a pattern round the pot;
He creates crevices that make it distinct;
He curves a mouthpiece for water's entrance;
His work is not performed by chance.

I am the clay.
My need to see the finished product
Only when the Potter deems fit.

I am the clay.
My desire and longing to participate
In the moulding process may be uncalled for.

I am the clay.
My belief to trust that the Potter knows the quality
Of His clay and will do a perfect work.

I am the clay.
My realization that the Potter can choose
To surprise me with the end product's outcome.

I am the clay.
Glimpses of this work I have seen,
Yet my joy at seeing the final product in full view.

Reflection Corner:

Imagine having a wonderful dinner by the sunset, engrossed in the panoramic views. You cherish every moment and you wish it would linger a little bit longer. The air is cool and the breeze is softly kissing your face in the company of loved ones. The delicacies to eat are large, and the colours are beckoning the eyes to look. You all start with your soup to warm your gut and then you eat some nice and fresh salad. Some olive oil is on the table. You take it and pour a generous amount onto your platter. Then you realize; a fly that failed to swim back to life while in the oil makes a portion of your dish. Your face cringes immediately and you are tempted to just kill this untimely creature, yet it is already dead! Your joy is drowned, at least for a moment, and your appetite weeps a while. What do you do when there is a fly in the ointment?

80. THERE IS A FLY INSIDE THE OINTMENT

There is a fly in the ointment;
Through the glass visible and transparent;
This fly contaminates the content;
The effects are obviously prominent.

In the ointment the residue lingers
Even though you try to remove it with your fingers.
The neck of the bottle is too small;
Don't use your own force, the bottle may fall.

Sin is flying in the backyard of many a heart;
The scum loiters of its mirth and dirt
Contaminating the pure oil of His righteousness.
Let Him deliver you from the filth of wickedness.

Your hand is too small for your rescue.
The majority cannot save you, neither can few.
To Him hand over your heart's bottleneck;
He will break it, your challenge to Him but a speck.

He will refill your bottle with His perfume of love.
He will mend the pieces of your broken self.
His view is eternal, majestic and above.
Trust His supply even when you can't see beyond.

Let Him remove and bury that fly.
His fragrance will surround you on life's aisle.
And when you think it's painful and you sigh;
Know that His store supply never runs dry.

There is a fly in your ointment;
God wants to relieve you from this torment;
Breathe freely of His power;
His grace is sufficient every hour.

The windows of grace He will open
If you let Him your heart's doors soften.
The refreshing air of peace will descend;
To His fields ripe, your feet He will send.

Reflection Corner:

Words are building blocks, and today, we have various forms of media where words are used. It seems that the social media would lose her breath were we to depend on pictures only; yet how sometimes we use them as tools for demolishing one another's strength and faith when the source of the Word is none but God Himself (John 1:1). Oh that we would use words as building blocks to strengthen the walls of another's faith; to help measure the depth of another's trials that we may come in and share a timely block of words to bring healing to the soul. These shared blocks will create a strong foundation in the life of the believer; supported by the beams of other's pillars as together we stand strong.

81. WORDS ARE BUILDING BLOCKS

Words are the deep and penetrating roots
Upon which an encouragement stands;
To bring soothing and healing to a hurt
And send a message of hope for a heart.

Words are the upward stem
That supports the continued growth
Of the Christian tree,
And gracious fruit bring forth.

They are the branches that hold
The failing and discouraged twig,
Giving strength to tender leaves
And the aged leg.

They help the plant to stay deeply rooted
In the soil of spiritual health.
The air of the Holy Spirit;
The constant and satisfying breath.

The bright petals to bloom forth
In resplendent beauty,
Ascending to the eternal
Blissful and magnificent city.

An influence sweet; an impact visible
On countenances and demeanours.
Oh Christ the power invincible;
Thy glory to finally see.

Help me to weigh the weight
Of each word that I speak
That I my not regret
When a heart in pain leaks.

Let my words;
Their roots be found in Thee;
Watered by your Holy Spirit,
My heart fully set free.

Reflection Corner:

The marriage institution (the union of male and female) is a school whose founder and Principal is God. The location is here below and the curriculum is the Bible. Through its sacred pages we learn many comprehensive lessons; one of which is God's desire for us to be healthy (3 John). The husband has specific responsibilities, and so does the wife. In our reading today, we hear about what joys there are for a wife in the home. Yes, it involves the sacred, often neglected simple tasks of cooking and cleaning, but we must never forget that these tasks performed in humility and love for one another, are holy and raise a tune of joy among the heavenly hosts.

82. THE JOYS OF BEING A WIFE

One of the joys
Of my sweet and simple life;
Is God's calling upon me
To be a godly wife.

Together with my beloved Husband
We make a godly home
Even as we wait
For our Master to come.
In the meantime
I enjoy the food we eat;
It keeps us physically
And spiritually fit.

And God has always continued
To give me the wisdom;
To prepare simple, nutritious,
Tasty delicacies with great aroma.

It's wonderful when my Hubby
Is always eating something new;
The gentle assuring smile
On his handsome face;

And how God's provisions
Have never been few
As He guides us
Through life's phases.

It's awesome when friends
And acquaintances share
The tastes in their mouths;
None to compare.
Thank you Jesus!
I am in heaven's kitchen! Let me to your voice
Always listen!

Reflection Corner:

The pathway of pride is filled with huge rocks of self that not only cause a painful stumble, but a deep and fatal fall. Pride can kill! It wraps itself in very subtle and seemingly innocent garbs, but to the one whose heart is being fashioned by the Designer, it is easier to catch the loose thread of pride, it's dangerous but tiny lace wrongly woven in the garment of character. We need discernment to tear it off that the garment may not lose its strength and Christian elasticity. Oh pride, so subtle, yet the consequences so visible; so empty inside, yet so full of self. It was "you" that led Lucifer to fall, and "you" have not left our midst, so to our Source of humility we must run that we may be covered and protected from this malady found in self.

83. MY DEATHLY PRIDE

Subtle in form it seems.
Often creeping our space in tiny streaks.
Beams of darkness usually hard to see;
Yet full of death as dark as it can be.

Clothed in false humility it approaches
The heart to faithfully train and coach;
A love of self to each moment propose;
Internal eyes glued inward, none to oppose.

Hiding in smiles and utterances
Of the achievements and holy providences;
Yet the truth is masked in ugly internal interferences;
Blocking pathways of growth and eternal entrance.

Oh pride, thou art folly.
Oh pride, pretend not to be holy.
You are from the devil.
You are full of evil.

Oh pride, thou art deathly.
You make the human being a weakling;
Comparing oneself with another;
From the pulpit of God we draw away further.

Oh pride, you enter the human heart stealthily;
You leave a stench that isn't good and healthy;
Corroding the humble veins in our core;
A loss indeed to the human race and a sore.

Oh pride, leave me alone!
My Master must teach me His word to hone.
God I ask you with true humility grace my heart;
Let me not the things of this world lust.

Oh pride, you always go before a fall.
Lord, let me hear your voice that calls
Me away from the dangers of this monster;
Draw me to your everlasting holy altar.

Oh pride, leave me alone!
My Humility Teacher says I can
With Him be one,
It's time for you pride to run!

Reflection Corner:

Purity remains a most prized possession regardless of the standards the media and fashion magazines set. Purity cannot be paraded on the temporary aisles of this world's entertainment; neither can it be boxed within! Purity has a way of finding her way out of the heart into the words and actions, and her motives soon become clear that they are pure. In a world gone wrong; where sex is reduced to an affair; a momentary pleasure—God is still in search of young people who are pure in His sight. He is interested in purity of body and purity of mind, for the body and mine sympathize one with another. What is your choice young woman/man with regard to purity? This piece is dedicated to young women/men, but it is fully applicable to the married and all singles. Find true purity from the wisdom of Him who has never sinned.

84. PURITY, YOUNG WOMAN/MAN!

Purity young woman/man;
Yeah, I know you can see the woman/man;
Yet I beg you guard your God given armour;
Do not yet ring the personal alarm!

Purity young woman/man;
Premarital sex is not fun.
Don't carry a bag of painful regrets.
Forsake a life of fear and dirty secrets.

Purity young woman/man;
From the loose one speedily run.
In carefulness keep off danger;
Where is God's pointing finger?

Purity young woman/man;
Are you willing to learn?
Then stop on your tracks and listen.
Accept the truth of God your life to glisten.

Purity young woman/man;
Novel books of fantasy reading burn.
A path of danger they pave.
Study God's word and you will be brave.

Purity young woman/man;
Watch what your eyes behold.
Your mind in His word hone.
You will experience joys untold.

Purity young woman/man;
Your body is God's Holy Temple.
Treat yourself with utmost care and concern.
Nothing vile its chambers to tamper.

Purity young woman/man;
In the strength of God you can
Keep thy body pure and holy.
You will escape earth's follies.

Purity young woman/man;
Heed the calm words of God's Son.
Ready are His hands your heart to guide.
No matter your sinfulness, do not hide.

Purity young woman/man;
Listen to His sweet tender call.
He alone is the One
Who guards your path lest you fall.

Purity young woman/man;
Is your source of purity the Son of Man?
Then latch your heart on to the hem of His garment.
He will save you from lust, pride and all torments.

Purity young woman/man;
Is the key to your conscience door in the Mighty Arm?
Pure thoughts and words shall fall from your lips
If you give Him your time, talents and gifts to equip.

Reflection Corner:

Walking can be fun. For those in the habit of taking walks, it becomes a joyful experience that one would not want to miss; yet it depends on your distance and the comfort of your shoes or lack of it. All walking, ultimately, ought to lead us to a desired destination. The sceneries may not be the greatest but the air and the winds, and even sometimes your own thoughts, can make a huge difference in the quality of one's walk. Today, the media highlights lots of stories about royal families. How about walking the royal road paved by the Master's hand, and have the Angelic Broadcasting Corporation proud to present the news to Jesus about us on the walks we have each day? Walk the Royal Road.

85. WALK THE ROYAL ROAD

Walk the royal road;
Stained with Jesus' blood.
This road may be rough;
But let Jesus be your touch.

This road is narrow;
Sometimes gravelled with sorrow.
But upon the royal road walk;
You will hear His voice talk.

Walk the royal road friend;
You will feel His hands torn.
A crown He will adorn you at the end;
You are not alone.

Walk the royal road, ye youth;
The big path of earth is not smooth.
Work the royal road on bended knee;
His purposes He will open your eyes to see.

Walk the royal road brother;
You will learn peace as you go further.
Walk the royal road sister;
You will not be bitter.

Walk the royal road church;
Souls to His kingdom you'll win much.
This royal road has the steady Rock;
The one that demarcates boundaries.

Walk the royal road paved;
By the pierced hand that gave.
You may hear human voices mock;
Yet to eternity you are headed with the Rock.

He gave His life for you and me,
That we may become a new!
He longs for us His face to see,
And our lives be fully renewed.

Reflection Corner:

Children are often referred to as precious jewels in many circles and churches. Their innocence remains unhidden and their high level of trust for older people is admirable. Watch a child cry one minute due to a strong admonition received and fall in the arms of the reprove at the next minute. They do not have a sense of pride like adults do. They are trusting and easy to please. Oh, what if we maintained that childlike faith that we may remain as precious jewels in the sight of our Father. He loves each child and desires that each will grow to adorn the mansions He has prepared for us. Be a precious jewel in the sight of our Lapidarist. He will be honoured by your faithfulness and commitment to shine for Him.

86. PRECIOUS JEWELS

When to you we fix our gaze
It is well;
For you make us shine ablaze;
Our voices your goodness to yell.

Make me glitter in darkness
Like a precious stone.
Show forth your glory in brightness
As I stand before your throne.

Let the eyes that see me
Behold your face of perfection.
My heart redeem
That I may inherit your salvation.

Look to my insides;
See the work you have wrought.
Beaten upon the earth's tides;
I am curved and taught.

Smile with me my Heart-smith;
Curve my shapes to fit your heavens;
Remove any leftover filth;
Make my life a blessed haven.

Call upon me them to comfort
Those that seem distraught;
That they may find your resort;
Heaven, a wonderful place aloft.

We are your precious,
Treasured jewels,
In your hands joyous;
Our eternal holy fuel.

Reflection Corner:

I only met her once as I ran along the trail, but what amazed me most was her willing friendship towards this stranger that I was to her. A tiny little baby girl she was with powerful lessons. Hands have been outstretched to this stranger separated from her Father due to sin. These hands continue to beckon me each day to come and hold His. Many times I want to run away because I think I have seen better, but I forget that the hands that want to hold mine are eternal, though once pierced by my sins. These hands have a warm embrace of love for all seasons and are powerful always to save me from danger. Thanks to this little girl who taught me a strong and powerful lesson on trusting God's hands.

87. POWERFULLY TINY

I beheld as I jogged on my usual trail;
This time not a dog's tail
But a gentle hand
From my newfound friend.

She had not for long lived;
Tiny baby girl, my soul to hers cleaved;
"Hallo," she said, as her hand she stretched;
Her love for me, not farfetched.

She is but a glimpse
Of gentle hands guiding my limbs;
As on life's trails I daily walk
And we spend time to commune and talk.

I looked up the sky, asking His plans;
Tender hands that hold onto my frail ones.
He sent this gentle hand, me to awaken
To the reality of His love that always beckons.

Lord, I cling to your gentle hands to guide.
In you alone can my deep heart confide.
When on these trails I journey,
Let me see the life's Son shining.

This gentle hand soft to touch;
Your love for me none can match.
This is not a trail of competition
But your veil open for contemplation.

Gentle hands, accompanied by a smile;
You say to me, "Hold on a little while;"
And as I journey through these miles,
Each day, your number I will dial.

Gentle hands guiding me at a tender pace;
I know I am not alone on this race;
And though I cannot see your loving face,
I am assured of your presence, your amazing grace.

Reflection Corner:

In construction work, the foundation and the pillars are most prioritized because the rest of the weight of the building rests on these two. Without a pillar, a building cannot stand. Pillars also determine how high or how low a building can go. So, I turn to the tallest pillar I know. His name is Jesus, and when He is present in our homes, schools, work, and governments, then we can be sure we not only have a sure foundation, but that our foundation is deeply held by strong pillars that will withstand any insurmountable pressures from external forces. As we invite this Pillar in all our affairs, we will see not only growth but also maturity.

88. CHRIST—THE PILLAR OF ALL STRUCTURES

Jesus, you are the pillar;
The pillar of all structures;
Erect, firm, stable, a holy altar;
Leaning on you, I am healed of all fractures.

To the individual may you be the guiding pillar,
That stands as the landmark,
Helping decisions to make clear,
As upon society, we endeavour to make a mark.

To the family may you be the loving pillar,
Teaching members each other to love;
Strong and firm, you the heart healer;
Our eyes to fix on Thee above.

At the school may you remain the pillar;
Students to seek you for direction,
Cultivator of character, heart tiller;
Show each willing one holy innovation.

At church, be the standing pillar;
The solid Rock on which we stand.
Against the mighty foe, the killer;
Guide us with your mighty hand.

At play, remain the joyful pillar;
Teaching us how to score life's goals.
Winning or losing, you are the dealer;
May we learn from life's moments foul.

In business, be the shining pillar;
Attitudes to keep sober, safe and clear;
Economies and profits, remove the chill;
Peace and contentment place in hearts without fear.

In our governments, be the conscience pillar;
Reigning over decisions, strategies and plans;
Positions of leadership, you are the filler;
Caring for all regardless of the clan.

I can lean against Thee strong.
In peace I find safety in your shadows.
Hold me straight; erect in readiness for the song
That we will sing by the beautiful river meadows.

I retire from life's familiar landmarks.
You welcome me to your eternal ark.
In communion together you and I.
My focus remains on you, the All seeing-eye.

Reflection Corner:

Each passing day brings us closer to our next birthday and closer to the grave if we sleep before the coming of the Lord. One day the candle of hope will stop blazing her flame; and the wax that has long enjoyed the glitter will lie cold on the tables of time. Will the vision of the flame have stayed in the minds of those who sat under its warmth? Will they be prompted to show forth kindness? To showcase eternal love? To exude gentleness, and to look above? What kind of legacy do you want to live? What kind of legacy do you want to leave? There is a time for everything, and the question is not that we will die, but what legacy we have left behind. We ought to be so bothered with sin that when it begins to linger, our conscience and the voice of the Holy Spirit in us will recognize it and help us deal with it.

89. LEGACY MOMENTS

Legacy, legacy.
What a word?
My history;
Not another fashion fad.

To Live an exemplary, fulfilling life;
To conscientiously walk a long life's ways
As one imbued with purpose and supremacy
For the things that last for eternity.

To Examine my motives and virtues
Through the eyes of my eternal Hero.
What's good, what's meaningful, and true?
I need not live my life on gear zero!

To remain Grateful for the opportunities;
Spheres of influence I have had to impact;
Another's life to fill with heavenly bounties;
My Lord to keep my spiritual sanity intact.

To Anticipate the joys and the sorrows,
To learn from today and tomorrow;
My Legacy Ladder I grow as I climb,
My life of everlasting realities, a future not blind.

Counsel I must with others share;
Encourage them, their mantles to wear;
Maximizing the talents and gifts,
Using these, another's burdens to lift.

Youth and tenderness fruits will not last;
In maturity I learn lessons through my past,
When upon His throne my crown I cast,
Having escaped the world and its lusts.

Reflection Corner:

A golden thread on a piece of fabric is attractive to the human eye. The glitter that comes with it embeds a price tag in our minds and we value it as great. There is a piece of thread that remains golden, though to this earth He came and marred His gold with our filth that we may learn to reflect His ambience and light. This piece of thread was brutally injured at Calvary. He could have broken the chains that bound Him to earth, but He chose to hang on in pain so we could learn to lean on Him for an eternity of joy. This is the thread that I want to encircle me. This is the thread that I desire to weave my character for the loom of heaven reaches to all willing hearts. Weave your character upon me; thread from heaven.

90. THE GOLDEN THREAD

The golden thread;
By your hands woven;
Your goal to spread
This heaven's love token.

Woven from Genesis to Revelation;
Not a sign of any confusion.
Each strand of your Word
In golden ways makes the sad heart glad.

This thread with holy blood stained;
No traces of the cheap blood of Cain;
Strong and everlasting,
Withstands any human stretching.

Thread woven by hands pierced;
This cursed piece of clay to be blessed;
Thread tied in hope from heaven to earth,
Guiding my feet on this chosen narrow path.

The gold in the thread tried at Calvary
Shines upon me with joy and sympathy;
Stretches forth through the garden of Gethsemane,
That He may forever bind in closeness you and me.

This thread visible in wooden shape,
The voice that cried, "*Eloi*" no human could tape.
This thread today carries heavenward my prayers;
Entangles the schemes of the evil slayer.

The thread in trinity, many represented.
All colours, one human race He calls to repentance;
My heart and yours must be contented;
This thread is not a mere happenstance.

From the foundation of the earth He was
A man of sorrows and on a specific cause;
Still loosening the thread of bondage
That ensnares many in this day and age.

Oh that this thread would jerk my feet;
Awaken me from spiritual slumber and defeat;
Feast at the Table of my Life's Weaver,
Each strand and pattern in me from the Life Giver.

Golden thread, remain visible in my dimming eyes;
Let me see your connections, how each piece lies.
Continue to repair my heart's broken pieces;
Stitch me that I may with you and others live at peace.

Reflection Corner:

Recently I met someone who said to me, «Religion is one big hell of a myth.» If someone told you that to your face, what would you say? As she discussed various religions with me, and I listened intently and gave her feedback, we connected at a point when she said, "her body is God's temple." "Do you believe in God?" I asked. "No, I don't." She replied; with all her energies from *"her body which is God's temple."* Meanwhile, I am uncomfortable being the Christian. (2 Corinthians 4:5, 6).

91. THE UNCOMFORTABLE CHRISTIAN

I am uncomfortable being the Christian;
Content church doors to walk through each week;
Yet passing others by on life's' daily streets;
Unconcerned about their sense of purpose and destiny.

I am uncomfortable being the Christian;
Satisfied to pray for the unevangelized,
Yet afraid my neighbours' doors to knock
With the urgency of Present Truth and His sweet sounds.

I am uncomfortable being the Christian;
Happy about my knowledge of the Good News;
Yet hugged by fear, unable to another explain my joy;
Barred by conquerable humanistic attitudes often coy.

I am uncomfortable being the Christian;
Content physical needs to provide for the poor,
Yet leaking in content from the Bible;
Unsure how to feed others with spiritual food.

I am uncomfortable being the Christian;
Rejoicing in offering prayers for the sick
Yet bypassing great opportunities;
Natural remedies of healing to teach.

I am uncomfortable being the Christian;
Keeping the cold ones on the streets warm;
Yet ignoring the obvious visibility
Of Him who can clothe all with His righteousness.

I am uncomfortable being the Christian;
Bound by doctrine and the great laws;
Yet depleted of love for one another
And heartless when others make mistakes.

I am uncomfortable being the Christian;
Focused on church traditions;
Yet when questioned what Jesus would do,
Lack Bible references to point others to.

Reflection Corner:

We love hiking, and as we climb higher and higher on the mountain and forest trails, there often comes a sense of exhilaration, not only brought forth by an increased supply of oxygen and a beating heart, but also by the ambience and beauty of the surrounding giant trees and the singing birds. Climbing is something we do every day on our spiritual journey, and as with forest or mountain climbs, we stumble and fall, but we do not stay on the ground. We can only afford to stay on the ground when on bended knees in penitence and prayer to the One who made the mountains and the forests. So, in life, keep climbing! Think of Jesus and His ascension; yet His humility will bring Him down again as He comes to take us higher. Keep climbing friend. Keep climbing.

92. I AM STILL CLIMBING

I am still climbing;
I am still on this distant path;
Rugged it seems to the eye looking,
Yet a path charted on this earth.

Sometimes my pace picks up;
Sometimes I stumble and fall down;
Yet the secret lies in looking up,
For then on this journey I continually go.

On my climb many trees I see;
Leaves are blown and tossed by the wind.
On the slopes are pebbles and some portions deep,
Yet my prize I must climb in order to find.

The mountain ahead of me is gigantic.
The storm often strong yet also majestic;
For when I am hot from the sun's rays,
My burning brow He soothes and on the path I stay.

As my climb I take each moment;
I've found the secret to relief from torment.
My hands must firmly onto the Rock clasp,
And stopping I must His Living Water to sap.

With each step higher;
My destination gets nearer.
Courage my soul to embrace,
As I prepare to see my Guide's face.

With my view fixed on the Prize Giver,
Relief from weariness comes easier;
For the Giver of all life's gifts
Has promised eternal life for me.

Soon I shall an inhabitant be
Of the New Jerusalem;
As I reflect upon my journey,
His eternal embrace of me are solemn moments.

Reflection Corner:

Many times in the course of the year we have opportunities of cherished moments with friends and family in our homes and outdoors. These are times of joy and reminiscences. For now, take a look through your window and see a face—It is the face of a human being like mine, like yours. This face has no joy; it is the face of grief. This face sheds tears of pain and uncertainty about the next meal, and cringes at the impeding night of cold on the street pavements. Would you this day, give joy to this grief stricken face? The face of grief is that of every human being. Regardless, all losses come with pain and grief has a face. The face of grief is that of every human being. Joy has a voice; grief has a face.

93. GRIEF HAS A FACE

Grief has a face.
It is the face of an unborn child
Struggling to keep her space
When mother aborts her into this world wild.

Grief has a face.
It is the face of a little boy,
Longing for the love of a father
Who has left home with an attitude coy.

Grief is the face of a little girl.
Heartbeats of fear hastening to find
Her lost identity and misplaced purpose,
Yet to many she is considered guile and a nuisance.

Grief is the face of troubled minds of parents;
Sleepless in the night as the thoughts wander
About the lives of their children and their whereabouts;
This important cause the heart never ceases to ponder.

Grief is the face of a spiritual leader.
It is the face of a Pastor
Exorcising demons from a believer,
Hopeful in the power; dependent on the Master.

Grief is the face of fear written on the bodies of the homeless;
Finding shelter under bridges and broken branches of trees.
It is the face of judgmental passers-by, who think these careless,
And the night's dark creates the umbrella of a shade and breeze.

Grief is the face of the malnourished and hunger stricken.
It is the groan of the weak muscles of energy depleted;
The flat stomach where the intestines themselves have eaten,
Yet a hope that may be today, bread may drop from heaven.

Grief is the confused and agonizing face of a street child,
Scattering city dustbins hoping for treasures to find.
It is the eager hands that lack the creative purpose,
For which work was made for the heart to blossom.

Grief is the rushing blood to the face of an orphan;
Longing for an embrace, a touch and care;
Unsure of what the future plans are for such a one,
Yet the heart beats with hope that help will come.

But Jesus has the face and loving eyes;
Winking with hope, grace and mercy,
Joining in the soul's laughter with cheer,
For unto Him these faces remain dear.

Reflection Corner:

Endurance! It implies stamina; the gentle force of what is achievable with an extra ounce of energy. It is fortitude, and it is also staying power—the ability to keep going when going seems not worth pursuing-nearly impossible. Endurance is patience—waiting with hope that the answer will come in response to an exercise of faith. This is the well marked path for the Christian. It is a path hewn with stones that may cause one to stumble, yet for the Christian; God positions these stones to raise us to higher heights. The path is marked, and we need not get lost.

94. ENDURANCE IS THE WELL MARKED PATH

Endurance is the well marked path of the Christian:

It is a path strewn at various intersections;
With pebbles of doubt that the feet of faith scatter;
With thickets of uncertainty that the flowers of grace uncover;
With rocks of surety that the sun of righteousness beams upon;
With sands of time that spread on the Christian's moments;
With the winds of life that blow each day to count.

Endurance is the well marked path of the Christian:

Patented with footsteps of movement in the will of His direction;
Hands of strength straighten the path for the sojourner towards the destination.
Eyes of love guide my footsteps at each step.
Ears of peace listen to my heart's cry at each point.
The aroma of His presence fills my air space with joy.
I look up to see the star of gladness beaming from a far.

Endurance is the well marked path of the Christian:

At ground level is the foot of the cross.
There I sit at His feet and deep lessons fathom.
A ground it is, watered by blood from His side.
Sprinkled by the pain of love towards me;
Sands of patience demarcate the cross's environment.
And His pierced hands beckon me "come."

Endurance is the well marked path of the Christian:

Petals of fallen flower stream this pathway.
The Rose of Sharon fell way below to our level.
We trampled upon He who came our souls to rescue.
His anger lasted only a moment and now His favour eternal.
The Rose's aroma permeates all of earth's corners.
The one who longs for the constant supply of this sweetness will linger with Him forever.

Endurance is the well marked path of the Christian:

Here the winds of Calvary blow to find room in souls.
Here stones of the thunder of forgiveness pelt sin's presence away.
Here the sunrise of God's love gladdens the pathways to the heart.
Here the moonlight of earth's midnight shines brightest in beauty.
Here the mountain's peak is the place I long to be.
Here I have a steady climb towards the New Jerusalem.

Reflection Corner:

Living with purpose gives one eager footsteps for going places; not for oneself but for the benefit of others. As we go places, we stop to ask about the end of the journey because we have a destination in mind. Nevertheless, before the journey ends; should we have lived purposeful lives, we get eager to show others the paths we have been on and the lessons we have learnt. We share with others what challenges we faced on those paths and the strategies we used to conquer them. That is legacy—living beyond ourselves; living in readiness for the world to come and when we leave, our presence will still live. It is a life that death cannot destroy, for death is but sleep. Consequently, when the time comes for us to sleep in the grave, it is but a time of sadness and joy, for the mourners know that death is not the end. What kind of legacy do you want to live and leave?

95. LEGACY

The kind of legacy I want to live and leave is one:

Where mourning and celebration kiss each other;
Where joy and pain dwell together;
Where loss and gain share the same space;
Where good deeds remain when the last breath is exhaled;
Where peace reigns and dances with turmoil;
Where love conquers hatred and wheels of reconciliation are oiled;
Where tears of joy and of agony are stored in the same bottle;
Where thanksgiving for life mingles with regret for life's loss;
Where lack of words fills many pages;
Where a statesman mingles freely with laymen;
Where one man becomes a relative to all mankind;
Where family is not restricted to blood relations;
Where the foundation laid stands erect on the hearts of many;
Where young children share in memories that hold true meaning;
Where a single soul touches the hearts of all;
Where vision breaks through beyond me to touch many generations;
Where words remain insufficient to express the true heart's content;
Where liberation breaks chains of loneliness
And weaves moments of reflective solitude.

The kind of legacy I want to live and leave is one:

Where true sacrifice and genuine service dwell within a frail human body;
Where passion precedes personal comfort for the sake of humanity;
Where death is faced with courage and absolute preparation;
Where the fear of death leaves so the joy of living is received;
Where the battery of breath is dead but the torch of freedom shines bright;
Where a bright rainbow breaks through amidst heavy storm clouds;
Where painful days of fighting bring years of continued healing;
Where a fallen spear is used to remove internal wounds;
Where memories seen in pictures remain stored in minds;
Where letting go leads to receiving treasures;
Where acts of goodness tip the scales of evil and conquer well;
Where holding out a hand of friendship attracts enemies to join in peace;
Where the road to justice is paved by shovels of utter patience;
Where prison doors open treasures to gladsome pathways for many lives;
Where courage runs ahead to remove the roadblocks of fear;
Where revolution breaks and buries the strands of superstition;
Where the balm of comfort is needed to soothe all humanity;
Where history is not past but remains in our present even tomorrow.
Where a man's inspiration lives beyond his present moments.

Reflection Corner:

The sight of blood is one most people do not appreciate very much. Our present media outlets fill with scenes of blood and these cause many a heart to be sad. This is because blood is meant to work its work by remaining invisible. It needs not be exposed for it to perform its duty. In fact, the moment blood is exposed unwillingly, like in accidents or abnormal bleeding; we know automatically that something is wrong. We however quickly forget of the one Bleeding Victim, who allowed His blood to flow willingly, that He may transfuse His life into us. He emptied Himself of life that we may live forever. Meet the Bleeding Victim.

96. THE BLEEDING VICTIM

The bleeding victim
Is dropping sweats of blood;
Symbols of His love these are;
His brow is covered complete
By sin's pelting hard,
But only for a moment.

This victim is innocent;
No judge can find reason
For any accusation,
But His heart is penitent
And in sorrow in need
Of consolation.

This victim has a wound
In His heart
Which no human doctor can treat
Except the victim's Father
Who upon this earth
The victim did send for our sake.

The victim's hands bleed
From the piercings
Of sharp nails
Yet on the cross He spreads them
And echoes His untiring voice loud
Saying, "I love you this much."

The victim's feet
Are trapped onto old wood,
Upon which His holy body lay;
Feet that once trod this earth
Many a lost soul did find
And to them brought salvation.

The victim is wearing a crown,
Not a kingly one depicting authority,
But one made of ugly thorns and agony,
One cast upon His gentle head by force;
Forces that He will soon defeat
When He finally wears the everlasting crown.

The victim's side is wounded,
Thrust and bleeding
Caused by ruthless men
That He once created to dwell
With Him in peace and harmony;
Yet freedom of choice He never denied them.

The victim's words are life
To any that is willing
Upon His counsel to take heed;
Upon His promise to stand up for;
Upon His precepts to obey;
Upon His example to follow;

Upon His law to walk by;
Upon His love's embrace to accept;
Upon His character to behold;
Upon His chastisement to welcome;
Upon His sacrifice to meditate;
Upon His eternal throne to look forward.

The bleeding victim
Died for us,
Yet death could not lock Him
In the deepest of graves
For to that He has the keys,
And none else.

And so He rose again,
Never to die,
For death He has conquered;
That we through Him
Might live again
Never to die!
If only we believe!

Reflection Corner:

Since childhood, when the art of managing a pen between my fingers came in small doses only, I found it easy to use anything I came across; from crayons to coal to my brother's permanent markers. My journey in writing has continued to inspire my own heart as I hear the Lord whisper to my soul what to write. I am learning that as I obey Him in writing what He asks me to, I will never run out of ideas as long as I do as He says to me. He is a God of love and has given to each one of us a gift. My desire is to always use my gift for God's glory, and today, I am excited to share with you what this journey of writing teaches me.

97. WHAT WRITING TEACHES ME

Writing is a practice I do each day.
It is that outlet of the grace of God,
Poured to my mind in abundance;
That I may carry out His purpose.

As I edit my work and each piece;
I know that life is like a page;
And the lines are the days;
Filling the page with the click of time.

I cannot move to the next script;
Until the present one is in order.
So must my days be lived with purpose;
Each to count for things holy and higher.

Editing teaches me character lessons;
Those things in my life that must change;
The improvements I need to make
So that my life script will read better.

Spell checks are equally important;
For a wrong spelling changes the whole line.
My attitude each day matters;
For a wrong thought cherished is of damage.

I must share my writing with others;
My moments of time given to strengthen another;
It is never a waste when I give of myself;
For then I grow and create room for more growth.

I must write with a theme in mind;
For then my reader can follow my train of thought.
Themes are the goals I set for each day;
With the vision I run, no time to decay.

Backspacing; reflective moments are important;
The timely move when a correction must be done
Or else the lines of life won't flow smoothly;
Deep thoughts to ensure the scripts make sense.

Some pages must be deleted after expressions.
There are burdens that we can't carry forward;
For they make the new load heavier
And steal today's energies needed to make life lighter.

Sometimes I use capitals, sometimes small letters.
For the moments I need to be heard I need to repeat;
My thought patterns to echo more than once;
But sometimes one small expression is just enough.

I must continuously save my work;
Cherish the thoughts of things I did well;
A backup system of encouragement to create
To return to when I need some laughter and cheer.

A word overused can make the reader bored.
There are many options for finding new words
So I must take a break from my routine;
To find something meaningful to cheer me on.

My writing must be like leaves in summer;
The strong wind of good content blows
Each word to send to a soul in need of peace,
And my source? The One whom all things knows.

Reflection Corner:

This far I hope you have a stronger character foundation laid as I believe each piece has had a gem that you will cherish for the coming days. Our first foundation was laid when God breathed into man and he became a living soul. Our second foundation was laid at our conception, surrounded by the pillars of mother's womb, where we had time to grow "enough" to be able to face the world. Our third foundation was laid when we intentionally decided to follow our Lord in the path to His kingdom, and from this one foundation, the building stands strongest. Which foundation are you prioritizing right now? Are there any changes you may wish to make? Priorities matter.

98. FOUNDATIONS LAID

What is my foundation laid upon?

Is it on the Rock of faith unshaken?
Is it on the depth of grace unmerited?
Is it from the vales of mercy granted?
Is it by strong pebbles of love deeply dug?
Is it on firm forgiveness surrendered?

What is my foundation laid upon?
Let it be shaped and be dug deep
By the strong arm of the Carpenter;
Let the layers be arranged
By the gentle hands that were pierced.

Let faith be the plumb line
Used by the Author of faith.
Let the cement of steady growth dry firm
Upon the holy grounds of righteousness.

Let the walls be smeared
By the blood on Calvary shed.
Let the building rise above
The world and its mediocrity.

What in my foundation keeps it strong?
It is the Sun of righteousness
Drying the wet character portions.
It is the wind of the Holy Spirit,
Blowing down from the heaven's throne.

It is the beautiful flower of mercy
Adorning the building under construction.
It is the leaves of righteousness on the trees
Of the gardens of our hearts.

It is the moonlight of cheer
Upon the darkest of midnights;
When everything seems still,
Yet I can steal the peace of earth in rest.

Reflection Corner:

A needy and a wanting generation. Does that describe us today? We all have needs and wants—those deep longings that we desire to see accomplished. Sometimes the word "need" implies a stronger emotion than merely a "want." In this context, I am using "want" to express the longing of my heart. It is my prayer that you too will find the passion of Jesus and work in His kingdom to win souls for His glory. What is the one thing that you would not want to live a day without? Well, when we know who the Source of Life and supplier of our wants is, then it will be easy for us to prioritize our wants and needs and take them to the throne where they are sifted and only the best is given back to us.

99. I WANT

I want to rise above the world;
Not because I have innate powers
But because He whom I find in the Word
Lives in me and promises to take me higher.

I want to see beyond the present;
Not because of any excellent eyesight
But because the Author of vision
Calls me to share in His mission a great part.

I want to hear beyond the audible;
Not because my eardrums are clearer,
But because He who upon my heart whispers
Is a communicative God always near.

I want to patiently run the race;
Not because I have swift feet
But because He who walked these paths
Gives me the speed to conquer.

I want to smell beyond the present aroma;
Not because I figure out the source,
But because I am His fragrance
And He allows His aroma in me to spread afar.

I want to touch beyond the physical;
 Not because I have gifted hands,
 But that He imbues me with powers spiritual;
 Sending echoes of mercy and balms to soothe hurts.

I want to lead others with authority;
Not the kind that this world portrays
But one of patience and gentility
Just as Jesus Christ teaches me daily.

I want to pray with fervency;
Not because I am gifted with eloquence,
But because the Holy Spirit prays through me
Uttering our petitions to the throne with divine urgency.

Reflection Corner:

I saved this long piece for mothers especially. This is the longest of the poetry inspirational pieces in this little book. I hope that this far you have enjoyed this 99 day journey knowing more about Character as He desires of us. I know some of us are mothers, and some are mothers to be, but one truth cuts across the board—we all came from our mother's wombs. For nine months or so, we were sheltered from the dangers of our surroundings and fed from within. Dear mothers, your work is honourable in the sight of heaven, and as I continue to learn about motherhood, it all points me to the Original creator of all Mothers and how He has a plan for each face we see and each phase of life we live in.

100. THE FACES AND PHASES OF MOTHERHOOD

A mother weeps from deep inside;
Her tears flow and she cannot hide;
Helpless at the bedside
Of her grown son recently involved
In a road accident, followed by a brain surgery.

There's one thing she cannot do.
She cannot heal her sick and helpless one,
Yet a greater thing she must do;
Present her son to the throne
Of the Father above.

I wish her tears could wash
The son's pain away.
I wish her sobs
Could awaken him up,
Eyes to open.

I wish her agony
Could suddenly turn
To laughter so deep,
It cannot be contained
In a moment.

Yet these I cannot do.
But one thing I must do;
Present this mother's heartfelt prayers
To the throne above with earnestness,
As if they were my own,
For one thing I do know,
Our Father cares and hears.

A mother tightly cuddles her little toddler
Between her weak and weary hands.
His eyes are closed, as hers remain open
Upon her loved one to diligently watch.

I see big tears drop on his brow,
And I hear her gentle and disturbed breath.
His heart is infected, and he sobs
While attempting sleep between her tender arms.

I wish the strong cuddle could awaken
His weakened heart to strengthen.
I wish her opens eyes,
Would meet the joy of finding his open too.
I wish her tear drops would to this infection
Reach and cleanse as a healing balm.
I wish her sobs would turn his deep groans
To audible and joyous laughter.

But this I cannot do.
But one thing I must do;
Present this mother's heartfelt prayers
To the throne above with earnestness,
As if they were my own,
For one thing I do know,
Our Father cares and hears.

This mother tightly cuddles her sick toddler,
Yet a home she provides for her unborn baby.
Her tears create a stream upon her face,
Where the expectation of healing
And the joy of delivering new life meet.

I pray her emotions will not
Negatively affect the new tenant in her womb.
I pray her two hands
Will soon hold her two babies,
One healed and the other born.
I pray her crushed spirit,
Will meet the rush and joy
Of seeing both her treasures walk.
And her husband's big hands,
Will be available and strong,
To hold all of them close
In love and unceasing prayer.

I pray that her sorrow
Over her sick child,
Will meet the joy of healing,
And sorrow will die and be buried.
I pray her first touch
Of her new born
Will send a sweet note
To her heart;
A sweeter tune
As her older son
Finds a playmate
And a beloved sibling.

A mother's gates have been opened
At the close of the year,
And her new baby to this world
Has finally arrived.
She tells me of her physical pain,
Yet she can't stop talking
About her emotional joy:
No, she doesn't need to talk,
Her face speaks aloud with joy,
As she lies on her hospital bed.

I am soothed by the thought
That giving birth is not
A debilitating disease
But an ordained moment
Created by the Giver of Life.

I pray her wisdom to care for herself
In all spheres of her life.
I commit the growth of her new baby
Into the Giver's hands
For strength and total wellness.
I pray the baby's father
Remains priest of the home
Guiding these little footsteps
To maturity and to eternity.

A mother is walking
By the windy beach.
On her arms is her newborn
Gently covered.
I watch her persistence
In ensuring the child's safety
From the strong winds.
I watch her joy
As her smile reveals
The peace that the sweet little face
Shines upon her ambience.

I watch her face
The winds head on
So that her little living treasure
Will remain safely sheltered.

I pray for her strength
To shelter this growing soul
From the winds of earth's fallacies.
I pray for her gentle hands
To lead this cute being
To paths of righteousness.
I pray her joy deep
As she watches the growth spurts
In her baby, into adulthood.
I pray she remains stable and clutching
Onto the Rock of Ages-
And that eventually
She and her baby will arrive
Safely to our eternal destination.

A mother is studying
In preparation for her role
She is at the pre-natal school
Where the Giver of children
Is taking her through great lessons,
Even as He prepares her womb
As a temporary home for a new miracle.
Sometimes she gets anxious
About the future.
Eager she is to know
When the Lord will unwrap
This living and breathing treasure,
But as she leans on Him in great measure,
She learns to give Him
Her cares and He readies her heart
For the miracle in pairs.

I pray she has faith some,
Enough to tarry for the Lord's perfect timing.
I pray to Him she will always come
For timely and everlasting counsel.
I pray her patience for the days when
Things don't seem to go her way.
I pray her ambience upon
The waiting muscles of her face.
Looking forward to greater things
To expect.
I pray her wisdom
For eventually the time will come
When this child will exit
From her hiding place,
To remain visible to the eyes
Of the watching universe.

I pray her a praying heart,
One that will not coil
Because of hurt,
But in obedience will
Never cease to pray,
Never cease her part to play,
And for eternity, she and her family
Never to be counted
Among the outcasts.

A mother is excited
To break the news of the arrival
Of her long awaited miracle.
For a time she has been silent,
For the evil one did bury her first miracle
In the smelly wombs of miscarriage,
But the Lord has raised another son
To dwell in this home as a gift.

I watch her pictures in her social network,
And the wonderful son covers her pages.
His little feet and eyes make anyone smile,
And I can imagine his gentle coos,
As he longs too, for his needs to be met.

He is a complete human being,
One that the Creator knew
Before in his mother's womb
He was formed.
And now he is here to be seen.

I pray that soon,
There will be pictures
Of his baptismal day,
His public confession of You
As the Giver of life,
Not only physically,
But also spiritually.

I pray that soon,
There will be pictures
Of his education,
As the Great Teacher
Coaches him in life's school
As an instrument of use,
In His vineyard here below,
As He prepares Him for the above.

I pray for the parent's wisdom
To count the blessings
And name them two by two,
For the gracious Lord
Has given another portion
Of His token of love,
Yet a great responsibility
To chart the course
Of this little heart,
To be excited about
Things eternal.

A mother is worried
Over where her girls
Have disappeared to.
In this technologically hot climate,
She cannot reach them on her cell phone.
She is missing her prayer appointment,
For her girls she must find.
She is running in the dark,
With a speeding driver,
Trying to find where these souls
Are hiding.

Her heartbeats return to normal,
As she finds her treasures,
Quietly seated at a friend's parlour,
Plaiting hair and content
To be where they are,
Knowing that mommy
Would find them.

I pray her little treasures,
Will know the importance of prayer.
And that in their pride
To show mother how responsible they are,
They will have zeal and eager drive,
To shine the light of Jesus wherever they may be.
I pray for the mother,
That at the feet of Jesus she will find comfort
For the days when she will not
Be able to control her children
As they move to the wings of adulthood,
Where they will make their own choices.
I pray for this widowed mother,
That the Lord Jesus will remain
Her comfort, her husband and the father,
To these little girls,
And that in Him alone
All will find their needs met.

I pray for all mothers! I do.
I pray for me!
Pass me not Oh Gentle Saviour,
While on Mothers thou art calling,
Do not pass me by!

Reflection Corner:

Made in the USA
Columbia, SC
19 October 2022